THE VIRGINIA PAPERS
VOLUME 1

THE VIRGINIA PAPERS

VOLUME 1

Volume 1ZZ
of the
Draper Manuscript Collection

Transcribed and Indexed by
Craig L. Heath

HERITAGE BOOKS
2006

HERITAGE BOOKS
AN IMPRINT OF HERITAGE BOOKS, INC.

Books, CDs, and more—Worldwide

For our listing of thousands of titles see our website
at
www.HeritageBooks.com

Published 2006 by
HERITAGE BOOKS, INC.
Publishing Division
65 East Main Street
Westminster, Maryland 21157-5026

Copyright © 2003 Craig L. Heath

Other books by the author:

The Virginia Papers Vol. 2, Volume 2ZZ of the Draper Manuscript Collection
The Virginia Papers Vol. 3, Volume 3ZZ of the Draper Manuscript Collection
The Virginia Papers Vol. 4, Volume 4ZZ of the Draper Manuscript Collection
The Illinois Manuscripts: Vol. 1Z of the Draper Manuscript Collection
The George M. Bedinger Papers in the Draper Manuscript Collection
The Mecklenburg Declaration
*Georgia, Alabama and South Carolina Papers,
Volume 1V of the Draper Manuscript Collection*
South Carolina Papers, Volume 1TT of the Draper Manuscript Collection

All rights reserved. No part of this book may be reproduced or transmitted in any form or by any means, electronic or mechanical, including photocopying, recording or by any information storage and retrieval system without written permission from the author, except for the inclusion of brief quotations in a review.

International Standard Book Number: 978-0-7884-2442-4

INTRODUCTION

The *Virginia Papers* were collected and partly arranged by Lyman C. Draper with the idea of publishing a revised edition of the work of Rev. Dr. Joseph Doddridge, *Notes on the Settlements and Indian Wars of the Western Parts of Virginia and Pennsylvania, 1763-83* (Wellsburgh, Va., 1824). Draper contemplated adding to a reprint of Doddridge's book many facts of early border history in the Valley of Virginia, in the Greenbrier settlements, and on the upper Ohio River and its southern tributaries. The first volume of these papers includes memoranda and notes for the proposed new edition of Doddridge's *Notes;* copies of family letters, poems, and a biographical sketch of Dr. Joseph Doddridge; a portion of the manuscripts of Stuart's "Narrative of Indian Wars and Settlements" (published in *Virginia Historical Collections,* i; also in *Magazine of American History,* i), found among Dr. Doddridge's papers; the narrative of John Bingeman (1763); letters of a "Russian Spy," published in the Chillicothe, Ohio, *Gazette* (1825-26); an account of the captivity of the Doddridge children (1778); letters and an obituary of Philip Doddridge; an original Indian novel by Joseph Doddridge, called *Tutela*; and Draper's correspondence with Miss Narcissa Doddridge (1866-69) relating to the proposed publication.

A fuller description of the contents of these papers, gathered as Volume 1-16ZZ of the Draper Manuscripts in the collections of the State Historical Society of Wisconsin, is given in *Guide to the Draper Manuscripts*, by Josephine L. Harper (State Historical Society of Wisconsin, Madison, 1983).

Access to the contents of the Draper Manuscripts has been facilitated by the above *Descriptive List* and *Guide* and by documentary publications and calendars and their indexes prepared from portions of Draper's collection, as well as by the availability of the entire collection on microfilm. Nevertheless, obstacles to research in this important historical resource have remained, owing to its sheer size (491 volumes of largely handwritten documents and notes) and the lack of an index to most volumes. It is to help remedy these difficulties that the current printed transcription and index to Volume 1ZZ of the *Virginia Papers* has been undertaken. It is hoped that further volumes in this series will follow.

NOTE TO USERS

This transcription of the *Virginia Papers* was made from the 1980 microfilm edition of the Draper Manuscripts, Volume 1ZZ. Portions of the documents in this volume are illegible or poorly legible, owing to fading, staining, discoloration, tight bindings, or disintegration of the paper with loss of parts of pages. Where illegible, these portions (whether single words or entire passages) are indicated by ellipses (...); some effort has been made to interpret poorly legible portions, but the original manuscript or microfilm copy should be consulted for verification. The transcript should be viewed as an aid to use of the manuscript, rather than a replacement or substitute for it, and users are urged to consult the original manuscript or the microfilm in parallel with the transcript.

Document numbers/page numbers are handwritten on the pages of the original manuscript. These are indicated in brackets at the beginning of the text for each page in the transcript. In many cases, the beginning page of a document has a cardinal number as page number (e.g. [p. 69]), and subsequent pages in the same document have the same cardinal number with a superscript or subscript (e.g. [p. 69^1], [p. 69^2], etc.). Owing to the variability in length of text on the manuscript pages, no attempt has been made to correlate page breaks in the transcript with those in the manuscript.

The spelling, punctuation, capitalization, and grammar used in the original manuscript have been preserved so far as feasible. Dashes have generally been replaced with appropriate punctuation. In some cases, a word or phrase at the end of a line or page was repeated at the beginning of the next line or page in the manuscript; these repetitions are reproduced in the transcription.

The Table of Contents reflects Draper's division of the manuscript into sections; the section titles are either Draper's own or constitute a brief description of the section contents (e.g. "Letter" with name of addressee). Some further descriptions are included in the Table of Contents in small typeface after the titles; these were supplied by the transcriber for the reader's convenience.

Ownership of the Draper Manuscripts by the State Historical Society of Wisconsin, and the cooperation of the Society in the production of this volume, are hereby gratefully acknowledged.

TABLE OF CONTENTS

Draft title page of new edition of Joseph Doddridge's *Notes on the Settlements and Indian Wars of the Western Parts of Virginia and Pennsylvania, 1763-83*   1
Notice of intention by George Morgan to issue land warrants   2
Letters from Joseph Doddridge
  to Philip Doddridge, Feb. 23, 1820   3
  to his wife, Sept. 14, 1824   4
  to his wife, Sept. 23, 1824   5
  to his wife, Sept. 24, 1824   6
  to his wife, Sept. 27, 1824   7
Biographical sketch of Philip Doddridge   8
Remarks by Henry Lee on Joseph Doddridge's Memoir   10
Elegy to Eliza M. Doddridge   11
Elegy to R. Reeves Doddridge   12
Biographical memoir of Joseph Doddridge   13
Letter from Joseph Doddridge to Philip B. Doddridge, June 22, 1822   25
Extracts from Miss Doddridge's memoir of her father Rev. Jos. Doddridge   33[1]
Letters from Joseph Doddridge
  to his wife, Sept. 24, 1824   33[4]
  to his wife, Jan. 15, 1825   33[9]
Early history of Greenbriar County, Virginia   34
  including Lord Dunmore's War, the battle of Point Pleasant, events in the French and Indian War, and sketch of Gen. Andrew Lewis
Col. John Stuart's Narrative   35
Narrative of John Bingeman   36
Letters of a "Russian Spy"   37

Capture of members of the Doddridge family	39
Elegy to Elizabeth Doddridge	40[1]
Elegy to R. Reeves Doddridge	41
Letters from Philip Doddridge to Benjamin Biggs	
Aug. 10, 1796	42
Dec. 4, 1804	43
June 11, 1818	44
Invoices for cotton traded at Tuscaloosa Falls	45
Letter from Philip Doddridge to John C. Wright, Dec. 16, 1828	46
Obituary of Philip B. Doddridge	47
Tutela, an Indian novel	
Chapter 1	48
Chapter 2	59
Chapter 3	63
Contract between J. W. Fleming and Benjn. Russell	69
Notes and References for Doddridge's *Notes*	69
Invoices for cotton traded at Tuscaloosa Falls	77
Notes and References for Doddridge's *Notes*	90
American Express receipt	90[1]
Letters from N. Doddridge to L. C. Draper	
Nov. 27, 1866	91
April 11, 1866	92
May 19, 1866	93
May 2, 1866	94
June 9, 1866	95
Nov. 1866	97
Nov. 12, 1866	98
Dec. 13, 1866	99
Jan. 23, 1867	100
Jan. 30, 1868	101
April 6, 1868	102
May 12, 1868	103
May 26, 1869	104

June 28, 1869	105
Letter from George W. Remsen to L. C. Draper, May 20, 1869	106
Letters from N. Doddridge to L. C. Draper	
July 7, 1869	107
July 19, 1869	107
Memo from L. C. Draper to N. Doddridge, July 2, 1869	109
Membership offer in State Historical Society of Wisconsin	109[1]

[p. 1]
Draft title page

Notes
on the Settmt. & Indian Wars
of the Western Parts of
Virginia and Pennsylvania,
From the year 1763 until the year 1783 inclusive.

Together with a view of the State of Society
and Manners of the First Settlers of the Western Country.
By Rev. Jos. Doddridge, M.D.,

A new Edition with new matter prepared
by the author, together with a biographical
sketch, and notes and additions
By
Lyman C. Draper,
Secretary of the Wisconsin Historical Society,
and
Wm. A. Croffert,
author of Connecticut in the War of the Reblellion.

(Also, See blank=book on Doddridge.)

[p. 2]
Notice of intention

April 1, 1776, Col. George Morgan, as Secretary and Receiver General of the Land Office of the Grantees and proprietors of the Retribution Lands, now called Indiana, gave notice in the papers that he would be ready to issue warrants for the taking up of lands, to receive the price or consideration monay, and to grant patents or deeds of confirmation of the same, on or before the first day of next May, on the premises, for all persons who have made settlements or improvements before the first day of January last past, within any part of that tract of country beginning at the Southerly side of the mouth of Little Kenhawa Creek, where it empties itself into the River Ohio, and running from thence south-east to the Laurel Hill, thence along the Laurel Hill until it strikes the River Monongehela, thence down the stream of the said River Monongehela, according to the several courses thereof, to the southern boundary of the Province of Pennsylvania, thence westerly along the course of the said Province boundary line, as far as the same shall extend, and from thence by the same course to the River Ohio, thence down the said River Ohio, according to the several courses thereof, to the place of beginning.

"And the said office will continue open until the first day of January next, within which time all such settlers may, on application to the Land Office, have warrants for any quantity of land not exceeding four hundred acres, with the allowance of six per cent for roads and highways, at the rate of Fifty Spanish Milled Dollars, weighing seventeen pennyweights and six grains each, or the value thereof in current money of any of the Neighboring Colonies, for every hundred acres, and the allowance, without reserving any quit rent to them the said proprietors. The purchase money to be paid immediately after the return of the survey, or a bond and Mortgage on the premises, to be given to the proprietors for securing the payment thereof, with interest at five per cent.

"The actual settlers being thus first secured in their possessions, the unsettled lands will all be surveyed into lots of four hundred acres each, for the proprietors, and the terms on which they will be sold made public.

"The settlers of <u>Indiana</u>, and others, may, on applicetion to Mr. <u>Morgan</u>, view and Examine the title deeds of the propietors, and be furnished with attested copies of the Indian grant to them."

— <u>Penna. Packet</u>, Apl. 15, 1776.

[p. 3]
Letter from Joseph Doddridge to Philip Doddridge

(Copy)
                    Feby. 23, 1820.
To My Son Philip:
    Your letter of the 23d inst. did not come to hand till the day before yesterday.

I am glad to find that at length you have learned to rise Early, and are likely to acquire the habit of steady & faithful industry. These are things on which you know I always set an high value. The duties of human life cannot be discharged without them. It is a trait in the biography of every great and good man that he was an Early riser. Dr. Franklin very humorously made a long arithmetical calculation, the object of which was to show the inhabitants of Paris that an immense saving of expense might be made by using the light of the sun instead of that furnished by candles and tapers.

Had the Elegant phraseology of the Holy Scriptures been more familiar to the mind of that great man than it appears to have been, he would doubtless have concluded his masterly Satire on the morning nap by asking the question why we should purchase light at so dear a rate while the good providence of Him who said "Let there be light, and there was light." Give us that blessing "without money and without price."

It is a matter of no small satisfaction to me, that mine has been a life of labor, which although not profitable to myself in a pecuniary point of view, has nevertheless been of some use to my neighbors in several ways.

I hold it a correct principle, sanctioned by history and universal Experience, that a life of useful labor will find its remuneration sooner or later. The "answer of a good conscience" is the never failing reward of a well spent life; and this is certainly a blessing of the first importance to its possessor.

The imperial court of public opinion, from whose decisions there is no appeal, is often slow in making and publishing its decisions on human cha[acter]; but they are made and published at last, and hence a life of munificence to the world is sure to be followed [by] "a good name, which is better than gold"; & this Even as a family inheritance is certainly of no small value.

Three descriptions of interests are presented to the mind of man as attainable by "the hand of diligence." They are those of piety, morality, and the world. The two first are attainable, and may be possessed in defiance of "time and chance which happen to all men". Time, thieves, storms, tempests,

[p. 4]
Earthquakes, pestilence, war, and a thousand other unforseen and unavoidable casualties, render the allotment of wealth, notwithstanding all our Endeavors, Entirely problematical, and considering the fate of most of our wealthy families, and that their Estate seldom descend to the third generation, it seems to be of little importance whether it be obtained or not. It is therefore wise to "choose the good part which cannot be taken from us."

My comment on your text has been so long that I have scarcely left room for anything Else. No matter. No event worth relating has occurred here since the date of my last letter. The family are well. On the whole, I have had better health this winter than has fallen to my lot for many winters past.

Jos. Doddridge.

Letters from Joseph Doddridge to his wife

(Copy.)

Uniontown, Sept. 14, 1824.

Dear Wife:

We arrived at this place last Evening. At Brownsville I was requested to spend the Sunday in the church, Mr. Bausman and the Presbyterian Clergyman being absent. To this request I acceded, and held two services, besides assisting in the Sunday Schools. Last Evening I officiated here in the Court House to a very large assembly. Thus without any anticipation of such a character I have become a missionary.

When at Brownsville I put up with Col. Brashier, who appears much concerned about his business with Edward Duvall. He said the lawyer and Sheriff were "butting at him about the debt"; but no judgment has been obtained as yet. Yesterday I saw Lawyer Lyon, who is Engaged for Mr. Duvall. He informed me that the suit was brought in favor of two men in the State of Illinois with whom Duvall and his partner never had any dealings, and that the action cannot be Sustained. He further says that Col. Brashiers is not at present bail for Mr. Duvall, that the Court refused to accept the bail-bond from the Sheriff, and demanded the body of Mr. Duvall, and that therefore the Sheriff, and not Col. Brashiers, is liable in case of a judgment. Col. Brashier shewed me a letter from E. Duvall, stating his readiness to pay the demand in case judgment should go against him. From the character of Lawyer Lyons as an Attorney, I suppose that E. Duvall is in safe hands.

We shall set off &c

We shall set off this morning for Connellsville, and from thence to Sommerset by the Pennsylvania route to Bedford and then to Cumberland. We travel very comfortably, and have but little to pay owing to my clerical character. This suits very well.

Yesterday we visited one of the mineral springs of this country. It is five miles from Brownsville on the road to Uniontown. It is certainly good sulphur water. It has been attended this season by a number of valetudinarians, but there none of them there at present.

We amused ourselves very much during the journey of yesterday with the aspect of the Laurel Hill: At first it appeared like a blue cloud; by degrees as we approached nearer we began to distinguish its different peaks, then its trees and "bald spots" as they are called.

Rezin still complains a little, tho' he appears to me much better than when we left home. He eats as heartily as I do, and sleeps much better. The gloomy prospect of death which has so long hovered over my mind begins to vanish. I have exercise and something to engage my attention. It may please Providence that I may be an inhabitant of the world a little longer. If so, I must keep at work

[p. 5]
doing good, if I can, be the result what it may.

The first evening after we left home I was much delighted with the surrounding scenery. The shady groves which skirted the road, the Evening songs of their feathered tenants, the fantastic figures of the surrounding clouds, tinged with a golden color by the parting rays of the setting sun on a dark base of vapour; but the Enjoyment was soon marred by the reflection — how soon will those senses by the means of which I hold correspondence with the beautiful scenery of Nature be locked up in death! How frail is philosophy itself!

My only concern is little Mary baby. Kiss her for me, and tell her papa will come back.

Jos. Doddridge.

Mrs. Dr. Doddridge
Wellsburg, Brooke Co.. Va.

(Copy.)
Bedford, Septr. 23, 1824.
Dear Wife:

We are here. Our progress has been but slow. In coming down the Chessnut Ridge, which is the first ridge of the Allegheny Mountains, the hind axel-tree of the waggon broke, the wood as well as the iron gave way. "Here we are" says Rezin. It was indeed a discouraging Event. I told him that our loss was not Equal to that of a ship with all its wealth and people; or to that of a boat on the Ohio or Mississippi, or Even a broken leg.

On the night before we had lodged at the house of a widow woman on the west side of the ridge. In the evening a Dutchman who lived about five miles on our route stopped at the house to wait for the rising of the moon to proceed with his waggon. We had agreed to breakfast at his house. I felt satisfied that this man could help us out of the difficulty. I walked the greater part of the road to his house, which was nearly three miles from the place of our accident. We found our landlord a smith and carpenter. He soon brought the waggon home. He and a hired man fell to work and spent the balance of that day, and the whole of the next, in repairing the waggon. The fore axel being ready to break, was replaced with a new one.

On Friday morning we got off for Sommerset. I began the journey by walking about six miles, four of which were from the bottom to the top of Laurel Hill. On the day of our mishap, I walked about the same distance, partly in going to see St. John's furnace, about two miles from our landlord's. This you will say looks like getting better; I hope so. Our good landlord took the waggon to the top of Laurel Hill with his own horse. His charge was five dollars, which I thought was low Enough.

At Sommerset I became a missionary again, delivered three sermons, and baptised three children, sold a number of books, and left some with uncle Wells' son-in-law, who by this time, I suppose, has sent you a paper.

The road by which we have come to this place is bad Enough; the greater part of it is what is called a "Mud turnpike", and was formerly pretty good, but the heavy rains this season have washed Every thing from it but the rough stones. The jolting of the carriage is terrible to Rezin, but not to me; I think I am the better for it.

Last Evening I officiated here in a Presbyterian church.

This morning I walked out to the Bedford Spring. It is a wild romantic place, but well fitted up with boarding houses, baths, and all other requisite accommodations.

This place and neighborhood is at present very sickly. Yesterday there were three funerals, and today one. This is occasioned by the great quantity of Stagnant water in the low vallies among the mountains. The Smell of this water often annoyed us as we came along the road.

Yesterday Rezin

[p. 6]
Yesterday Rezin received a letter from home dated the 14th. Mary was still unwell. I am in hopes she is better.

To-morrow I Expect we shall leave this for home by way of Pittsburgh.

Jos. Doddridge

Mrs. Dr. Doddridge
Wellsburgh, Va.

(Copy)
Bedford, Sept. 24, 1824.

Dear Wife:

We intend to leave this place this morning for home by the way of Pittsburgh. We shall travel the old Pennsylvania road by the way of Stoy's Town & Greensburgh. We shall travel but slowly owing to Rezin's indisposition. I think he is better than we left home, but he is anxious to return, and I feel it my duty to accede to his wish, altho' at present much against my interest.

My "Notes" are highly Esteemed, but owing to the poverty of the times I cannot sell so readily for cash as I wish. I have, however, disposed of a considerable number of copies, and a larger number I have deposited in Safe hands for sale. Were I alone, or with a healthy person, & with a good strong horse, I should go on and sell all my books, or nearly so, for cash; but I must submit to the present inconvenience, and I shall do it without a murmur.

Before I arrived here I intended to find, if possible, the house in which I first drank coffee; and, in the Event of finding it, I should have invited a few acquaintances whom I should make in the place, to take a cup of coffee in the same room. Remembering the name of my former landlord, which was Nagle, and being able to give a tolerable description of the house, on inquiry I was informed that Dillon's Tavern, the stage office at which we put up, occupies the site of Nagles' house, but the house itself has disappeared, and been succeeded by a large tavern edifice. "Sic transit gloria mundi."

Yesterday morning I walked out to see the famous Bedford Spring. It is about two miles from the town. The place is highly romantic, owing to the surrounding mountains, & decorated in a superb style, with baths, boarding houses and dormitories. The great hall for dances and other amusements presents many Superb and fanciful decorations. The chandeliers are beautiful. At a little distance from this hall, on a low piece of ground, stands a Naiad, a large half naked female figure, with a Grecian face and costume, on a pedestal of rocks, holding in her left hand a huge concha, from the top of which the water of the mineral spring spouts up to the height of ten or twelve feet; but, poor girl, her fine white drapery is all turning yellow by means of the sulphate of iron contained in the water which is constantly falling on it.

The Spring issues from the western side of the Cove Mountain at the height of nearly twenty feet above the creek which runs at its base. The Spring is large, and runs with great force thro' apertures between large rocks, which still retain their original situation and aspect. A few rods higher up there is another but a less Spring of the Same kind. The water of the large Spring is conducted into a large reservoir, which Supplies a long range of baths, which are filled at will by hoisting a little floodgate. The water in the baths is reached by a flight of steps. I had not the heart to make the descent. The side of the Mountain from which the Spring issues is [laid] out into serpentine walks for the benefit of walking, and Enjoying the Mountain air.

Those who attended the Spring returned home at an Early period than usual; and, no wonder, for this is at present "the valley of the shadow of death". There were two funerals here yesterday, and this morning I hear of two more for to-day. It is a discouraging ciircumstance that those who came here in quest of health while using the mineral water are doomed to inhale the pestilential Effluvia of the surrounding Stagnant marshes so as to risk their lives by laying the foundation for the worst of fevers.

I saw but one gentleman in attendance at the Spring. His aspect arrested my attention very forcibly. When I arrived at the place he was walking the long gallery of one of the boarding houses, with a slow, measured step; his countenance was intelligent but gloomy. He continued his walk without paying regard to my company or our entrance into the Gallery. He continued his solitary walk until I had found an Excellent harpsicord in one of the rooms adjoining the Gallery, and began to play on it. He then Stepped into the room, sat down, and listened with attention to the music. Never in my life did I so much wish myself a good musician. Had I possessed the power of pouring all the Sweet variety and captivating force of tune along the trembling strings, I should have done so until from the lineaments of his countenance I should have discovered that I had hit the key adapted to the Suspension of his Sorrows, and continued that as long as he should have kept his seat. Gladly would I have known the history of this man, but as he seemed averse to conversation I offered him none.

This may have been right; it may have been wrong. On inquiry concerning this man, all I could learn was, that sometime ago he arrived here from the Saratoga Springs. In dress and otherwise, he appeared to be in no want of the things of this world. It is his heart which suffers, but from what cause I shall never know.

I have been Examining the oldest records of this court for the names [of my ancestors], and only find that in the year 1771 my grandfather was foreman of a grand jury at one session of the Court. Being within ten miles of the place of my nativity, I wish to see something concerning my father's title to the land on which he lived in Friends' Cove, but could find nothing, as his title, whatever it was, originated while this county was a part of Cumberland County. It is said here that the land is now owned by one Cisney, and that he cheated my father out of it. So it seems I am not the first Doddridge who was liable to the imposition of sharpers, and yet my father was a good man.

I have visited the court house here. It was built in the reign of his Majesty George iii. The edifice is of stone, and, without Exception, the most misshapen, sombre, disgusting public Edifice I ever saw in my life. I do not think that the Bastile itself could possibly have had a worse

[p. 7]
appearance. I took my seat for a moment on the bench of justice, and after looking round for a moment on the antiquated, ill-shapen jury boxes, counsel tables, and filthy and disgusting [floors], I gladly made my Escape from the forum of my forefathers.

Tell Narcissa that I have dined here with a lawyer Bird whose wife was Miss Waugh, a former acquaintance of hers, & that She desires to be affectionately remembered to her and yourself. She appears to be in very ill health.

I think I am in much better health than when I left home. I am stronger, and do not cough so much. Publick Speaking, I find, instead of hurting, benefits me. I have preached only once here. There are but few Episcopalians in this place.

I have written you this long letter not only for your amusement but for the purpose of preserving the impressions made on my mind by what I have seen and heard in this place.

Jos. Doddridge.

Mrs. Doctr. Doddridge,
Wellsburgh, Va.

(Copy.)

Greensburg, Septr. 27, 1824

Dear Wife:

We are here from Bedford. Our March has been very slow over the mountains along the roughest roads.

The day before yesterday at half past eight we reached the top of the Allegheny, which where the Pennsylvania turnpike crosses it is very high. The view from this Spot, both East and West, is truly sublime. The ranges of mountains both ways seem to rise in Succession behind each other, until the farthest seems to lose itself in the horizon. The pestilential vapors of a whitish color could be traced over the marshes from which they arise in the Great Valley which we had left behind us. The huge rocks, aged pines, and scub oaks around us had a venerable and Ever solemn aspect. The sound of the air through the tops of the pines is like that of a distant tempest. But I must stop, or I shall turn poet.

Our horse and waggon have so far held out very well. I think I am better. Some days I walk as many as six miles. Poor Rezin is much worn down, and complains a good deal, & no wonder, our road has been so rough that the jolting of the carriage is terrible to him, tho' not so to me.

We hope to reach Pittsburgh on Wednesday Evening. If this should reach you in time, Rezin would be glad if some of his friends would meet him there. He is impatient to see some of his people, and also to get home. I am so too.

Jos. Doddridge.

Mrs. Doctr. Doddridge,
Wellsburgh,
Brooke County,
Va.

[p. 8]
Biographical sketch of Philip Doddridge

Philip Doddridge, an American lawyer and politician,

born in _____ county, & year 1772, died in Washington, Nov. 19, 1832. His family were associated with the pioneer settlements on the Ohio river, and as a boy he worked with his own hands at the plough. But failing in health in consequence of severe physical exertion, he was placed at school when sixteen years of age, and made rapid progress in his studies. A too close application to his books having rendered it necessary for him to intermit his educational pursuits, and having been invited to join two or three young men of his own age, who were going to New Orleans with produce, he embarked with a flatboat, and floated down the Ohio and Mississippi. On reaching Natchez, then in the possession of the Spaniards, the young boatmen found the place under strict police regulations, which forbade the admission of strangers into the town; but Doddridge determined to take a walk around the Environs, and actually began to ascend the hill. Here he was met by an officer who addressed him in Spanish. Doddridge replied in Latin, and the Spaniard, who proved to be the Governor of the post, was so much struck with the learning of the manifested by a boy engaged in the management of an Ohio flat-boat, that he invited him to dine, and upon his departure gave him letters of introduction which admitted him into society at New Orleans. Upon his return home, he commenced the study of the law, and having entered upon the practice of it soon gained a local reputation, Especially as an advocate before a jury, hardly inferior to that Enjoyed by Patrick Henry in the tide-water portion of the commonwealth. He entered public life as a delegate from Brooke County, to the lower house of the Virginia Legislature in 1815, and continued for several years, at various times, to represent that constituency. But it was not till the Constitutional Convention of 1829-'30 had commenced its sessions, that the full intellectual Stature of the man was displayed. He was one of the members chosen for the district composed of the counties of Ohio, Tyler, Brooke, Monongalia & Preston, and one of his colleagues was Alexander Campbell, the founder of the religious sect known as the "Disciples of Christ." Mr. Doddridge was the acknowledged leader in the Convention of the party in favor of the white basis of representation, and maintained his ground in the great debate in which Randolph, Leigh, Upshur, Stanard, and Tazewell supported the other side. In this discussion, and the innumerable debates which sprang out of it, Mr. Doddridge was, according to Mr. Grigsby, the historian of the Convention, "a gushing fountain of facts and figures". He had few of the graces of the accomplished orator; his voice was not musical, and he had little skill in its management; in person he was of a short and stout stature; his features were immobile, even heavy; and he was singularly negligent of the proprieties of dress; so that his success in parliamentary conflicts was due to a close ratiocination, perfect knowledge of the subject, great energy of manner, and a wonderfuul command of terse, appropriate words. He was Elected to Congress soon after the adjournment of the Convention, from the Wheeling district, but his career was brought to a close before his first congressional term had Expired. At the time of his death, he was Engaged in codifying the laws for the District of Columbia as one of a committee appointed by Congress for that purpose.

[p. 9]
Doddridges Notes
Mann Butler, in his work on the Valley of the Ohio, speaks of the Notes as "the treasury" from wh. he

drew so freely in his acct. of frontier manners.

Phil. Doddridge died of apoplexy, in Wash. City, Nov. 19th 1832, in the 60th year of his age.

Lyman C. Draper Esq.
Baltimore
[postmark] Philadelphia Jun 17 5

Wm. F. Boone — Phila.
June 14, 1846
The Boones of Maryland.

[p. 10]

Remarks by the late Rev. Henry Lee, of the Ep. Ch. of Washington Pa., now decd.

Upon reading attentively the memoir left with me by Miss Doddridge, I would advise her to leave out the whole from page 4th commencing with the last paragraph "When the Methodist Society" &c to page 23. All this part of the M. relates so exclusively to the P. Episcopal Church, that the general reader would take little interest, and other denominations might feel and say, that they had been imposed upon, for they had been induced to subscribe for a history of the Early settlements and Indian wars in Western Pa. & Va., and not to the history of a particular religious denomination, &c.

I would advise the leaving out the minute statement of Dr. D's family, only stating the number of his children. I would leave out the latin quotation as too common. Something like this might close the Manuscript.

The readers of this short account of the life and

character of Dr. Doddridge will readily perceive that he was a man of no ordinary character. His native powers had been strengthened by studious habits, for his mind seemed to feel the usefulness, and the intellectual facinations, of literature and science. His natural quickness of observation had full scope and variety of subjects in actual life in the circumstances of the regions of country in which he was born, and of that in which he passed his life. His Early settlement in Western Virginia, and his constant travelling through Western Pennsylvania gave him an Extensive, as well as minute knowledge (in most instances, real personal knowledge) of the stirring and still deeply interesting history he has given of the Early Settlement and of the customs of that part of the States mentioned. His Notes, published in 1824, have furnished the reliable materials of their history, and have been referred to by every subsequent writer. The additions now to be made to the first Edition from his genuine papers, will prove highly valuable, as materials of the most authentic character for future histories.

    We would now leave the reader to proceed to the work before him, and may venture to promise him no ordinary gratification.

    Note. — Those subscribers and other readers who take a special interest in the Early condition and progress of the P. E. Church in Western Va. & Pa. will find these Subjects in appendix. In that they will see the disinterested, unceasing ministerial labors of the good and holy man, and will doubtless remember him with profound respect, while descendants of many frontier families will cherish the memory of this modern apostle in labor and sacrifices abundant, and almost "without measure".

An Elegy

On the death of Eliza M. Doddridge, who died January 11th, 1819, aged 15 years, by her father, Rev. Jos. Doddridge.

My dear Eliza! Thou art gone,
Thou sweet, thou lovely child!
Thy little span has quickly run,
And all our hopes beguil'd.

Why hast thou thus, impartial death,
Destroy'd so fair a prize?
Thy dart which laid her in the Earth,
Makes thousands bleed besides!

Thy lovely form, thy polish'd mind,
To all thy friends are lost;
Thy tender heart, and taste refin'd,
Are laid with thee in dust.

For thee no more thy garden flowers
Shall shed their rich perfume,
For thee no more thy garden bowers
Shall give their shade at noon.

No more thy song, no more thy lyre
Shall charm thy lov'd abode,
No more those eyes which sparkl'd fire
Shall beam on those she lov'd.

Thy deeds were good, thy faith correct,
And all thy thoughts were pure;

We lov'd thee much: can we regret,
Thy God has lov'd thee more?

Why have I learn'd that all must part,
And bid the world farewell?
'Tis now I feel death's fatal dart,
And breathe his gloomy spell.

Again! again! The gush of grief,
Bursts from the heart in tears;
Again! again! I ask relief,
But find no comfort near.

Let the companions of her youth,
Weep round her funeral pall!
Forget her not, tho' sunk in death,
For much she lov'd you all.

Thou shalt not leave me, No! my child,
My faith still claims thy cares;
Be thou my guardian angel mild,
In my declining years.

Well hast thou fled a world of pain,
Tho' sad thy parting knell,
So soon we all shall meet again,
We will not say <u>Farewell</u>.

Wellsburg, Va., 1819.

An Elegy

On the Death of R. Reeves Doddridge, who died in Chillicothe, O., on the 9th of January, 1825, aged

Eleven years.
> By his father, Rev. Joseph Doddridge

O! Strike ye angels, strike the lyre,
> And softly breathe your sweetest dirge;

O! Welcome to your heavenly choir
> The little saint you have in charge.

O! Sound your harps, ye heavenly band,
> And every voice the hymn prolong;

The portal past, in Canaan's land,
> He joins you in your holy song.

Blest be the hand which led my child
> Into the Sacred house of God;

The place with grace and mercy fill'd,
> The house of Jesus' blest abode.

Blest be the altar where he knelt,
> And pour'd out his soul in prayer;

Blest be the mercy which he felt,
> And wip'd away the falling tear.

He is not dead! Nay, but he sleeps!
> His cold, and dark, but hallowed rest,

O'er which his friends will often weep,
> Is with his angel's presence blest.

Yet Death stood by, his dart half drawn,
> This little saint is not your prey,

His angel said, "O! Death begone" —
> Then bow'd and kiss'd his soul away.

Biographical Memoir

Rev. <u>Joseph Doddridge</u>, M.D., author of the following graphic description of pioneer life, manners and

Indian warfare in the West, was the Eldest Son of John Doddridge and Mary Wells, natives of Maryland, and of English descent. Shortly after their marriage, which occurred Dec. 22, 1767, his parents removed from Maryland to Friend's Cove, a rich and fertile valley, ten miles south of Bedford, Bedford County, Pennsylvania, where the subject of this sketch was born Oct. 14, 1769.

Dr. Doddridge in reply to the inquiry of a friend, in 1821, who expressed a wish to be informed whether he was related to the celebrated English divine, Rev. Philip Doddridge, gave the following account of his ancestors:

"From all the information I have been able to obtain respecting my ancestors, I am led to the conclusion, that the father of the Rev. Philip Doddridge, and my great grandfather, John Doddridge, were brothers — sons of the Rev. John Doddridge, Rector of Shepperton, Middlesex County, England. My great grandfather came to American when quite a youth, and settled in the Colony of New Jersey. He left but two children, Joseph my grandfather, and a daughter, Ann, who married a Mr. Moore, of Maryland.

[p. 14]

"If the above genealogy be correct, and I have no doubt that it is so, the Rev. Philip Doddridge was first cousin to my grandfather. The former deceased in 1751, aged 50 years; the latter died in 1779, but he lived to be an aged man; so that the dates of their nativity could not have been widely different. I cannot learn that there has Ever been more than one family of the name of Doddridge, Either in England or in this country; and, so far as their history is known, they have at all times been a small family."

Early in 1773, John Doddridge, having lost his

farm in the beautiful valley of Friend's Cove, by neglecting to complete his title to a settlemenent right, removed with his family, and some of his neighbors, to the western part of Washington County, Pennsylvania, settling a few miles East of the line which divides that State from North-Western Virginia. Thus, in the fourth year of his age, the subject of this Memoir became a resident of the Western country at that interesting and eventful period when its primeval forests first began to be settled by the adventurous pioneers. The state of society, and the privations of the Early settlers during his boyhood days, are graphically related by his own pen.

[p. 15]
Losing his Excellent mother Nov. 20, 1776, when in his eighth year, by a wound from a horse, which resulted in mortification, his father soon after sent him to Baltimore County, Maryland, under the care of a relative, to attend school. Some of his experiences while on the way, and during his three years sojourn there, are delineated in his "Notes" as illustrative of the habits and customs of the people of those primitive times.. After his return, till he attained the age of Eighteen, he was occupied with his father in labors on the farm.

An incident is related on the authority of his sister, Mrs. Ellen Brown, showing that even in early life he cheerfully sacrificed his own comfort to promote that of a suffering fellow creature. On one occasion, after his return from Maryland, and when twelve or thirteen years of age, he was sent on an Errand in the neighborhood, in the month of December, when the weather was quite cold. He returned minus his coat, and upon being interrogated as to the cause, he hesitatingly replied that he had given it to a poor old man whom he met, shivering with ague, and destitute of any outer garment to protect him from the inclemency of the weather. So the young Samaratan, while conscious of having performed a good act, had to do without a coat until material for a new one could be manufactured in the family; for, in those days, there were no Stores at hand, where such goods could be procured.

[p. 16]

In Early life young Doddridge was brought under the influence of religious truth. His father, after his settlement in the West, united with the Wesleyan Methodist Society, then in its infancy, and differing little in its doctrines and ritual from the Church of England, to which he had been attached in his native State, and which had then no organization in the frontier settlements, nor for several years thereafter. Soon after identifying himself with this people, Mr. Doddridge Erected on his own premises a house both for public worship and Educational purposes.

The late venerable Rev. James Quinn, an Early and devoted minister of the Methodist connection, in his auto-biography, published in 1824, thus speaks of this primitive Edifice, and some of those who worshipped within its walls: "In Washington County, Pennsylvania, we next find our missionaries on the waters of Cross Creek and Buffalo, kindly received by John and Philip Doddridge, brothers, and their brother-in-law, Capt. Samuel Teter. These all, with the greater part of their numerous families fell into the ranks of Methodism; and Joseph, son of John Doddridge, became a traveling preacher of considerable promise and success, and the first in the Great Valley. But after Mother Church got ready, he went and took orders, got a black gown and white bands, and came out parson. On the land of John Doddridge was built a neat log meeting house, said to have been the first one Erected on this side of the Mountains. The Society, I am informed, has transferred its meetings to Middletown, midway between Wellsburg and Washington; hence, going East on that road, a short distance from Middletown, you leave on your right hand, within one mile, Doddridge's Chapel (This memento of John Doddridge's liberality, and of the interest he took in the moral and intellectual improvement of those around him, was still in Excellent preservation as late as 1862, and still retaining its original cognomen, and regularly occupied as a preaching station.), and the sleeping dust of many of the first members of the Methodist Society, in the head of the Great Valley. The Doddridge and Teter families, and the Society in their neighborhood — and I knew them

[p. 17]
well, more than forty years ago — were a noble, free-hearted set of Christian people, who loved one another, and served God with sincerity and humility of mind."

The late Hon. Thomas Scott, of Chillicothe, Ohio, who, in Early life, was an itinerant minister of the Methodist connection, states: "My first acquaintance with the Rev. Joseph Doddridge commenced in July, 1788, in Hampshire County, Virginia, at the house of the Rev. John J. Jacob. He was then in company with the Rev. Francis Asbury (It was at the instance of this good man, Mr. Asbury, that Dr. Doddridge made himself acquainted with the German language, and sometimes preached in it. His knowledge of the German was thorough, and highly valued by him in after life as a medium of communication with those who knew no other language.), by whom he was held in high estimation. A short time previous to our meeting, although not yet nineteen years of age, he had been received as a traveling preacher in our Society, and was then on his way to the Holston Circuit."

After about three years itinerant ministerial labor, he was recalled home, in April, 1791, by the death of his father, who had appointed him Executor of his Estate. These new duties, together with the unprotected situation of his step-mother and the younger members of the family, constrained him to suspend his traveling labors in the ministry — which, as the sequel will

[p. 18]
show, were not resumed.

Having settled the affairs of the Estate, and finding some available means at his disposal, he resolved to qualify himself more thoroughly for the responsible calling he had chosen, by devoting some time to perfecting his Education. With this object in view, he entered Jefferson Academy, at Canonsburg, a few miles from where he was reared, accompanied by his brother Philip, who had been from childhood his associate, laboring together by day in field or forest, and at night poring over books at the family hearth-stone. The late Rev. Robert Patterson, in 1852, thus communicated his reminiscences of the brothers while at Canonsburg: "It affords me pleasure to comply with your request respecting my Early acquaintance with the late Rev. Dr. Joseph Doddridge, for whose memory I cherish the most profound regard. Several years previous to 1794, I had been a student in the Academy at Canonsburg, and during a portion of this time he was there. We were room-mates, boarding in the family of the Rev. Mr. Mercer. David Johnson, the Principal, and the students generally, as is usual in literary institutions, soon determined the grade of his intellect, his moral character, and his personal worth; and none, during my connection with the Academy, stood higher

[p. 19]
than he in the Estimation of those who knew him. His brother Philip (A sketch of Philip Doddridge will follow this memoir.) was with him. Both were remarkable for original genius, intellectual strength, and close investigation of any subject that came before them. These qualities, combined with amiability of disposition and uprightness of deportment, Endeared them to both teachers and students."

Dr. Doddridge seems to have remained at the Academy at Canonsburg but a few months. During that period, however, he must have laid the foundation of a solid Education, judging from the results of his subsequent career. But he did not resume his ministerial labors in the Methodist Society, as they had seceded from the Mother Church; and the clergy had, as he believed, laid aside the prayer book, and departed in its public ritual from the usages enjoined upon them by their founder, Rev. John Wesley, to which, as well as to precomposed forms of worship, Dr. Doddridge cherished a decided preference.

He, therefore, resolved to take orders in the Protestant Episcopal Church. In March, 1792, he was ordained a Deacon, by the Rt. Rev. Bishop White, in Philadelphia. When he commenced his labors, in the service of the Episcopal Church, in Western Pennsylvania and Virginia,

[p. 20]
many of the scattered settlers, who were originally from Maryland, Eastern Virginia and the Carolinas, where they had been attached to the English church and its forms of

worship, gladly availed themselved of his ministrations. He had, as Early as 1793, two parishes in Brooke County, North West Virginia, in which small log churches had been Erected, and one at West Liberty, Ohio County, where services were held in the Court House. At the first of these parishes, St. John's, he continued his pastorate nearly thirty years, when declining health compelled him to relinquish it. Soon removing to the mouth of Buffalo, subsequently known as Charleston, & since as Wellsburg, on the Ohio, in Brooke County, Virginia, he Extended his labors across the Ohio River, preaching at Steubenville as early as 1796, and held frequent Services there for several years.

The people, however, at that Early day were poor, and their voluntary contributions afforded him but a meagre support. His amiable companion, when recurring to this period, would playfully say, that before her husband commenced the practice of

[p. 21]
medicine, he was too poor to provide himself a second suit of clothes; so when Saturday afternoon intervened, he was necessiated to remain incognito, while she adjusted his habiliments for his appearance in the pulpit on the coming Lord's day — not only the labor of laundress, but the skill of the seamstress, being frequently called into requisition on these occasions. Knee-buckles and long stockings were then in vogue.

In order to meet the wants of an increasing family, Dr. Doddridge found it necessary to combine with his clerical profession, one that would give promise of more of the comforts and necessaries of life in the region in which Providence had cast his lot. He chose that of medicine, and devoted himself to its study, completing his course of preparation in the winter of 1800, in the medical school, under the celebrated Dr. Benj. Rush, of Philadelphia. In the department of medicine, Dr. Doddridge became Eminently successful and deservedly popular, and the avails of an Extensive practice Enabled him to rear and Educate a large family of children.

He was admitted to the Priesthood in the Protestant Episcopal Church, in Philadelphia, in March, 1800, by the Rt. Rev. Bishop White. Though a resident of Virginia at this period, yet owing to the great distance of his residence from the Bishop of that State, and the diffi-

[p. 22]
culty at that Early day of holding correspondence with him, he continued in fact, though not canonically, under Bishop White's jurisdiction, with the consent of that prelate, and, accordingly, for a long period made all his official communications to him.

For many years his double professional labors steadily increased, in providing for the Spiritual and physical wants of the people. His whole ministerial career was practically a missionary one — preaching in the scatered neighborhoods and settlements, on both sides of the Ohio, for many miles around. In 1800, he formed the nucleus of the present parish of St. James, in Jefferson County, Ohio; & from 1815 to 1822, he held regular monthly services there. At St. Clairsville, in Belmont County, in that State, he formed a congregation, as Early as 1813, and, sometime after, one at Morristown, in the same county. He made a missionary tour, in 1815, as far as Chillicothe, officiating there, and in nearly all the intermediate towns going and returning; and during the autumn of the following year he made a tour to Worthington, Ohio, officiating Eighteen times during his absence — among other places, at Zanesville, where a church was organized, and he chosen the pastor of the infant parish.

[p. 23]
In addition to the churches to which he ministered in Virginia already mentioned, he had congregations at Wellsburg and at Wheeling; the latter he kept in Existence till 1820, when a resident pastor was settled there.

Dr. Doddridge thus concluded a letter to Bishop White, in Dec. 1818: "Last week I made a missionary Excursion of six days, in the southern parts of Belmont and Monroe Counties, Ohio, during which I held divine service seven times, forming one congregation in the latter county, and baptizing thirty children. I was told, that had not a mistake of one day occurred in the appointment, the baptisms would have Exceeded one hundred. Many of these people had been my parishioners previous to removing to their present locality, and, with their neighbors, had delayed the baptism of their children twelve years, in the hope of having that holy rite administered by a clergyman of their own church. This circumstance affected me deeply."

As an additional instance of the attachment of some of the Early settlers to the Church of their fathers, it may be mentiontioned, that, on one occasion, Dr. Doddridge was sent for a distance of seventy-five

[p. 24]
miles to preach the funeral sermon of an aged patriarch, who had, at one time, been one of his parishioners, but had removed some years previous to his Death. The aged man, before his departure, had requested that Dr. Dodd-

ridge be sent for, and that all his children — a numerous offspring — be gathered on the occasion; and the minister, after the funeral, be taken round the neighborhood and instruct them in the way of life. It is almost needless to add, that the good clergyman with sincere pleasure complied with the request.

Aside from his professional callings, Dr. Doddridge had other cares and honors thrust upon him. In 1812, he was chosen a corresponding member of the Academy of Natural Sciences, of Philadelphia; he was a member of the Masonic fraternity, and was frequently called upon by his brethren for public addresses; and for several years he held the office of magistrate in Brooke County, but finding it materially interfering with his clerical and medical duties, he finally declined further service in that capacity. In 1814, he accepted the appointment of chaplain and surgeon to a regiment raised in Western Virginia, designed to operate on the sea-board; but the news of the treaty of Ghent between the belligerent powers, however, was received before the regiment reached its destination.

"In the infancy of the Protestant Episcopal Church of Ohio", says Taylor's History of that State, "Dr. Doddridge's services as a minister of the gospel were cheerfully given to the settlements opposite Wheeling; but in 1820, he announces an intention of resuming the medical profession, as a means of acquiring a competency for his approaching age". But his toils in the ministry, and the fatigue and Exposure to which he was subjected in the practice of the healing art, unavoidable in a new and sparsely settled country, at length gradually undermined his constitution, not naturally robust, and Engendered a disease, from which, in his later years, he at times suffered greatly; its severe paroxysms being attended with

[p. 25]
great nervous irritability, depression of spirits, and a morbid sensitiveness, foreign from his character when in comfortable health — being then uniformly cheerful, self-reliant and hopeful.

The following familiar letter, addressed, June 22, 1822, to his Eldest son, Philip B. Doddridge, of Portsmouth, Ohio, Exhibits him in one of his happiest moods, in the midst of his simple domestic surroundings; and cannot fail to impress Even a Stranger with a most favorable opinion of his goodness of heart, and the natural playfulness of his disposition:

"It is now Early in the morning, and I am seated in the bower, which has been removed from the spread apple tree, to the shaded grass-plot nearer the house, at the request of your Excellent mother, who oftentimes has tea in it, and sometimes dinner. She has just risen from a night's repose, and looks young and blooming as a girl of Eighteen. She is now talking to the gardener, and, at the same time, feeding about fifty chickens, which are thanking her for her munificence in their noisy gabbling way.

"Many changes have been made here since you left us, an account of which will, no doubt, be acceptable to you. The foundry

[p. 26]
lot is converted into a first-rate vegetable garden. The old garden is enclosed in a new fence, six feet high, and finished with a coping. I have made a flower garden for S. It is tastefully laid out in circular beds, and, if well taken care of, and stocked with flowering shrubs and plants, will, in a few years, present a fine parterre of var-

iegated beauty. Gardener as I have always been, S. is the only one of my family who manifests a taste for this delightful Employment — in addition to which, I strongly suspect she is to be my prettiest daughter.

"The bees have all been removed to the new bee-house, which stands on the north-east corner of the lot below the turnpike. It is twenty feet long, and eight feet wide, built of brick, with a circular dome overhead, and plastered inside and out. The family vault, recently finished, is of the same dimensions.

"I am at present much amused with the playful gambols of some squirrels, which are frisking about, sometimes on the trees, and sometimes on the ground. About a month ago, I made a den for some of these little animals, into which I put several pairs. They now seem well satisfied; but will they stay, or decamp after some time? I am a Republican, and like pets, but not prisoners.

[p. 27]
I do not like to see a bird in a cage, or an animal tied by the neck.

"Joseph is still with Mr. Campbell, and is doing well. He is much beloved by his teacher and fellow students. It is my wish to make him a finished scholar. Reeves and Charles are fine little fellows. The latter has the character of a good boy. Reeves has a little of the Indian in him, but, I think, not so much as you had at his age. As you are a business man, and will probably become rich, I think you ought to take one of these fine boys, and teach him that which he will never learn from his father — the art, mystery, and trade of money-making.

"Mary baby has just risen, and come out to the bower. Dear little stumpy, her affection for me is sometimes almost troublesome, as her chief concern is to be with papa wherever she can find him. Your sister Harriet's health is poor at present; Mr. Duvall [her husband] is greatly alarmed about her. On the 24th inst. I am to deliver an oration for the Masonic fraternity at Brownsville, Penn., and shall take her with me. The journey may be beneficial to her.

"N. writes us, that your wife is very pretty; I trust that she is also very good. Do bring her to see us. My caugh has almost left me,

[p. 28]
and I am in very good spirits, as you will perceive from this long letter. May God bless you and yours."

Something of Dr. Doddridge's love of nature — flowers, bees, birds, animals — is strongly indicated in the familiar letter just cited. In horticulture, and the culture of bees, he found an interesting and agreeable relaxation in his intervals of professional labor. His garden and orchard, both of which were well cultivated, contributed greatly to his home enjoyments. The morning carols of the feathered songsters among the leafy boughs were, to him, sweetest music; and he was often out betimes, he said, "Mentally to unite with them in offering the matin hymn of praise to the Giver of all good." He would not permit one of these winged tenants of the air to be injured on his grounds, telling his children who sometimes objected to the birds having the finest cherries and other fruits, "that the same munificent Being who supplied them with food and clothing, provided also for the little birds, and if they came to his premises for food, they must not be molested." In his treatment of bees, he deviated from the mode then prevailing — that of destroying the little laborers, in order to procure their honey; and the success which attended his Experiments, proved that his views respecting

[p. 29]
the Economy and habits of these industrious and useful insects were not chimerical. He published, in 1813, a Treatise on the Culture of Bees, in which he gives a minute description of his Apiary, and details his plan of colonizing the bees, instead of killing them to obtain the fruit of their labor.

For many years, Dr. Doddridge had contemplated the design of writing a work on the Early settlement, Indian wars, and pioneer customs of the Upper Ohio Valley; and, ultimately, a more Extended production on the History of the Indian Wars, Embracing the whole scope of the Great Western Valley — which latter, he justly thought "would certainly be a valuable acquisition to our literature." The opportunities afforded by his Early and subsequent long continued intercourse with the first settlers — among whom he was reared up to manhood and spent his whole life — assisted by a habit of close observation, a tenacious memory, and the interest he took in treasuring up incidents illustrative of the times and character of those among whom he lived, pre-eminently qualified him for giving a truthful and vivid history of the country from its first settlement, as well as a correct account of the manners, customs and conflicts of

[p. 30]
those who labored to transform its interminable forests into fruitfulness and beauty. While he drew upon his own strong memory for the details of the primitive habits and customs of the country, he obtained from surviving pioneers and Indian fighters narratives of Indian warfare.

After about a year devoted to its preparation, the work which is here re-printed, Notes on the Settlement and Indian Wars of the Western parts of Virginia and Pennsylvania, was completed in 1823; but from an unavoidable delay in procuring the manufacture of paper, owing to the scantiness of water in the stream on which the paper mill was situated, the work was not published until the following year. Owing to ill health, Dr. Doddridge was unable to give the necessary attention to an Examination of the proof sheets, and consequently many errors escaped correction; and the same cause prevented a proper canvass for the work, so, on the whole, the issue proved an unprofitable investment to the author, while failing health, moreover, precluded all idea of the more Extended history he had hoped at some future day to prepare.

But though unfortunate, in a pecuniary point of view, to himself and family, the work, nevertheless, proved one of the most valuable additions ever

[p. 31]
made to the history of the Western Country; indeed, it stands 'solitary and alone' as the faithful Exponent of the simple modes of pioneer life in the Upper Ohio Valley. And to this unpretending volume will the memory and fame of the author be almost Exclusively indebted for their preservation from that forgetfulness and neglect which ordinarilly fall to the lot of men. Some of the more important testimonials of well-known border writers as to the worth of Dr. Doddridge's historical labors, we venture to subjoin:

"The book before us," says Hall, in his Sketches of the West, "is the production of a reverend gentleman, who was reared in the wilderness, and was intimately acquainted with the whole subject on which he writes. His father came to Western Virginia in 1773, during the deceptive calm which preceded the rupture of 1774, usually called Dunmore's war. Brought up in the wilderness, the inmate of a cabin, Dr. Doddridge spent his whole life in the midst of those dangers and vicissitudes which make up the life of the borderer, and has detailed a variety of minute circumstances, which render his book Exceedingly valuable."

"A most interesting sketch of the manners and customs of the times, written very generally with graphic Effect," is the Estimate of Butler,

[p. 32]
the historian of Kentucky; and in a magazine historical series, he refers to the "Notes" as "the treasury" from which he drew so freely in his account of frontier manners. "This is a valuable little work", asserts Monette in his History of the Valley of the Mississippi; while Howe, the author of the Historical Collections of Virginia and Ohio, pronounces it "an interesting and graphic Volume". Sherman Day, in his Historical Collections of Pennsylvania, says: "It is pleasing, after the revolting details of frontier warfare, to contemplate the more peaceful and convivial scenes of the Early pioneers, as drawn by the graphic pencil of the Rev. Mr. Doddridge". "None", says De Hass, in his History and Indian Wars of Western Virginia, "but one who had lived among them, shared with their wants, and suffered with their privations, could accurately describe the varied and peculiar life of the old pioneers. We have Every reason to believe, that the account of Dr. Doddridge is, in the main, correct."

Rev. Dr. John M. Peck, one of the most discriminating of Western writers, observes of Doddridge's Notes: "This is a curious and interesting little volume,

Especially as giving us a most graphic picture of the state of society and manners of the first settlers of the Western country." James H. Perkins, the able author of the Annals of the West, thus gives his impressions in a paper on the Literature of the West, in the October number of the New York Quarterly Review, 1839: "Many years since, a little volume was published by Doddridge, which is well known to all students of Western history, as being one of the most genuine, accurate, and full pictures of the first settlers, among whom he was brought up". And other Western historians, and writers upon border Events, such as Jacobs, Withers, Kercheval, Stone, Drake, Schoolcraft, Parkman, McDonald, Mayer, Hildreth, Howison, Craig, Collins, Dillon, Taylor, Hart, and Hartley, Either cite Dr. Doddridge as authority, or quote from his Excellent work.

[p. 33[1]]
Extracts from Miss Doddridge's MS. Memoir of her father Rev. Jos. Doddridge

That part which I have not already re-written down to the issue of his Notes, 1824 — L. C. D.

His views of life — its purposes & duties were just & liberal, drawn as they were from the Bible, general Experience and observation. Regarding man as amenable to his Creator for the due improvement, and practical Exercise, of the talents committed to him, he Endeavored by a life of active usefulness and uniform Christian effort, to discharge his obligations to God & his fellow men.

Some years after he had taken orders in the Episcopal Church, he found it necessary in order to meet the wants of an increasing family &c. studied medicine, went to Phila. & attended medical lecturers in 1800 &c. Then follows:

Previous to this time he had formed a matrimonial connection with Jemima, orphan daughter of Mr. John Bukey, who had, in 1791, Emigrated from New Jersey to Western Virginia. Mr. Bukey died some years after his arrival in the country, leaving a widow, three sons & four daughters, the youngest of whom at the age of sixteen became the wife of Dr. Doddridge. Mary, the Eldest daughter, was the wife of Majr. John McColloch, of Short Creek, Ohio County, Va.; Maria married Col. Harmon Greathouse, of Lexington, Ky: Two of the sons, John who married a daughter of Maj. Wm. McMahon, who fell at Fort Recovery in Aug. 1794, & Hezekiah, son-in-law of Col. Joseph Tomlinson, of Grave Creek, were at an Early age spies under Capt. Samuel Brady, of Indian war notoriety; Rudolph, the youngest son, settled in Shelby Co. Kentucky, where many of his descendants reside.

[p. 33[2]]

He never laid aside that simple unpretending manner, unostentatious style of living & open hospitality which characterized the pioneer society in which he had been brought up, & which, in these respects, he thought superior to the manners and Etiquette of modern days.

He was simple in his tastes, and moderate in his habits, discountenancing both by Example and precept the indulgence or cultivation of a fastidious appetite.

His colloquial powers were good. He was easy of access, fond of innocent anecdote, & possessed in an Eminent degree the faculty of accommodating himself to the peculiar tastes amd capacities of those with whom he conversed. He was fond of children, who always received from him a kindly greeting, and they, in return, loved him.

For laboring people & servants, he had much consideration, always giving them a kind and cheering word indicative of an interest in their welfare. Hence, with these classes, he was very popular. Indeed, throughout life, he was Emphatically the friend of the poor.

In his disposition he was cheerful and social; in his habits industrious, temperate and domestic. When in health, he always rose at four o'clock, devoting the morning hours

[p. 33³]
to meditation and literature. To those who trimmed the midnight lamp, & indulged the morning slumber, he would say in the Elegant phraseology of Scripture: Why should you purchase light, when the Good Providence of Him who said 'Let there be light, and there was light', gives you that blessing 'without money and without price'.

His benevolence, like that of the good Samaratan, was Exemplified in acts of kindness to the poor and the afflicted, to whose relief he liberally contributed of his limited means: On some occasions, where the sick were destitute of friends as well as funds, removing them to his own house, where they gratuitously received the benefit of his medical skill, together with such other appliances as their comfort and necessities required, until restored to health.

He was Enthusiastically fond of music, the science of which he perfectly understood; & having a fine voice, he generally led the chants and singing in his own congregations. When at home, his evenings were often spent with his family and students in the practice of this innocent and rational recreation, both social and instrumental. He never taught his children but two songs: Hail

Columbia, & Erin Go Bragh. Being a patriot, he taught his children to sing the inspiring song of "Hail

[p. 33⁴]
Columbia; & possessing a feeling & sympathising heart, he taught them to sing the plantive air and words of Erin Go Bragh.

His published writings, in addition to those already mentioned, were "Logan, the last of the race of Shikellemus — a dramatic piece"; "Dialogue between a Dandy and a Backwoodsman"; & sermons and orations on special subjects and occasions.

In the winter of 1823-4 he completed his arrangements for the publication of his Notes &c.

In Septr. of this year, (1824,) he set out on a journey Eastward, having a two-fold object in view: the improvement of his health by travel, and the disposition of some of his books; but owing to the indisposition of his travelling companion, he went no farther than Bedford, Pa.

The following letter to his wife, presents a brief review of some of the incidents of his journey.

Bedford, Sept. 24th, 1824.

We are here. Our progress has been slow, but I think my health is somewhat improved. I have Enjoyed the journey greatly. The scenery through which our route lay is characterized by a quiet beauty, Except in the mountain regions, where it is distinguished for grandeur and Sublimity; but while gazing with admiration upon these displays of the Creator's power and goodness, my pleasure was suddenly checked by the reflection that those faculties by means of which I now hold communion with the beautiful in Nature, must soon be closed in death. But thanks to the Great Author

[p. 33⁵]
of All, I am Enabled by faith to look forward to a world where beauty, peace & purity are Eternal — where none shall know pain or weariness, such as I now feel.

"At Brownsville, Uniontown & Somerset I was invited to preach, which I did — at the latter place baptising two children. Thus, without expecting it, I have become a missionary.

"Before arriving here (Bedford), I intended, if possible, to find the house in which I first drank coffee, in 1779, & in the Event of finding it, to invite a few friends to take a cup with me in the same room. Remembering the name of the landlord, Nagel, and being able to give a tolerable description of the house, upon inquiry I found that Dillon's Hotel, at which we were stopping occupies the site of Nagel's house.

"Yesterday I went out to see the famous Bedford Spring. It is about two miles from town. The site, owing to the surrounding mountains, is highly picturesque and romantic. The buildings of this watering place consist of baths, boarding houses, and dormitories. The great hall for amusements presents many fanciful and gorgeous decorations. On a low piece of ground, some distance from the hall, on a pedestal of rock, stands a Naiad, a large half-naked female figure, with a Grecian face and costume, holding in one hand a huge condia, from the top of which the water of the Spring is thrown upward to the height of ten or twelve

[p. 33⁶]
feet; but, poor girl, her fine white drapery is losing its original purity of color by the action of sulphate of iron contained in the water which is constantly falling upon it.

"The spring issues from the side of the Cove

Mountain, nearly twenty feet above the creek which meanders at the base. It is large, the water flowing with great force through apertures in immense rocks, which still retain their primitive situation and aspect. A few rods higher up is another but smaller spring.

"The water of the principal spring is conducted into a large reservoir, supplying a long range of baths, which are filled at pleasure by raising a small floodgate. The water in the baths is reached by a flight of steps.

"The side of the mountain from which the spring issues is cut into serpentine walks for the convenience of pedestrians who wish to take Exercise and inhale the mountain air.

"I have been Examining the oldest records here for names of my family, but have found only that my grandfather Joseph Doddridge, who is mentioned as foreman of a grand jury in the year 1777.

"Being within ten miles of the place of my nativity, I wished to learn something concerning my father's title to the land on which he lived in "Friend's Cove", but could find nothing as his title, whatever it was, was granted when

[p. 33[7]]
this was a part of Cumberland County. I have been told, that the farm is now owned by a Mr. Cissna, and that my father was unjustly deprived of it, but by whom I have not been informed.

"The Court House here was built in the reign of his Majesty George III. The Edifice is of stone, and is without Exception the most mis-shapen, sombre looking building I ever saw. I do not think that the Bastile itself could have presented a more forbidding and gloomy aspect. I seated myself on the bench of Justice, and after taking a survey of the antiquated ill-shapen jury-boxes, and council table, gladly made my Escape from the forum of my forefathers."

Soon after his return from Bedford, he received a letter from Bishop Chase, just landed in America after his first visit from England to solicit funds to aid him in carrying out his Enlarged views relative to the Missionary and Educational interests of his infant diocese — announcing his arrival at Kingston, and appointing the 3d day of November for a special meeting of the Diocesan Convention of Ohio, at Chillicothe, and Expressing a hope that he would meet him there.

This Convention Dr. Doddridge resolved to attend, and taking with him a little son, Eleven years of age, he proceeded by Easy stages to Chillicothe, and during the sitting of the Convention he accepted, at the request of the parish of St. James,

[p. 33⁸]
at Zanesville, a missionary appointment to that place.

In consequence of the impaired state of his health, he had some time previous relinquished the charge of his parishes in Virginia & Eastern Ohio, and from the same cause he had been counselled to discontinue the practice of Medicine in a vicinity [region] where attention to its duties involved Exposure to the vicissitudes of the weather, & the necessity of being on horseback much of the time.

By restricting his labors to the parish at Zanesville, with proper care, he fondly hoped to regain a portion of his former health and vigor; but He in whose hands are all our times ordered otherwise. For some months he was able to attend to his parochial duties; but in the Spring he had a severe attack of pneumonia which brought him to the brink of the grave.

After recovering some strength, he wrote to one of his friends, saying:

"My life is fast ebbing away. I cannot promise myself a single day beyond the present. <u>The prospect of death is now familiar to my mind, and it is by no means unpleasant.</u>"

To his other afflictions this winter was added the loss of his little son, who had accompanied him to Chillicothe, & whom he had left there at school. On that melancholy occasion

[p. 33⁹]
wrote to his wife as follows:
Zanesville, Jan. 15th 1825.

"Before this reaches you, my dear wife, you will probably have received the sad intelligence of the death of our dear Reeves, who died last Sunday evening, after a few days illness.

"My niece, Mrs. Collins, in a letter to me, after giving the particulars of his illness, & death, says:

"But, dear Uncle, with this painful intelligence, I have joyful news to communicate. During the Month of December last, God graciously revived our Church — the Methodist — with an unusual out-pouring of his Spirit. Reeves attended all the meetings with us, because deeply interested, and was soon a bright Example of the power of converting grace. His intelligent prayers and conversation astonished all who heard them. When I told the dear boy that his physicians were afraid that he would not get well again, a heavenly smile overspread his countenance, & he said with much animation, "Then, dear cousin, I shall go to my precious Savior", and continued calm & happy till he gently fell asleep in Jesus."

You may remember the deep interest Reeves always seemed to feel in things relating to God, and how anxious he always to go to church and hear about Jesus. We little thought then that his Heavenly Father was preparing him for so Early an Entrance into his kingdom. Precious

[p. 33[10]]
as he was to us, we must no lament his loss. Considering the ills of life, we ought to console ourselves with the reflection that our dear boy has been taken from the Evil to come — that he safely garnered up in heaven, where, through the abundant mercy of God, we may hope soon to meet him.

When the weather became settled in the Spring, Dr. Doddridge, being no longer able to perform parochial duty, left Zanesville to visit his Eldest son in Fayette County on his way spending several weeks with his sister, Mrs. Nathan Reeves, in Chillicothe.

We again quote from Hon. T. Scotts reminiscences:

"Prior to the renewal of my intercourse with the Rev. Dr. Doddridge, in 1793, he had taken orders in the Prot. Epis. Church, and now had charge of several parishes in Western Virginia. At West Liberty, in Ohio County, I occasionally attended upon his ministrations.

"When preaching, there was nothing in his manner that savored of pedantry or rusticity. He spoke fluently, and was perfectly self-possessed; yet he did not possess that graceful action and delivery often met with in speakers in Every other respect his inferiors. These apparent defects, were, however, amply compensated by the Earnestness with which he enforced the truths of the Gospel, the purity of his style, and the substance of his discourses.

[p. 33[11]]

"In person, he was tall, but muscular and well proportioned; hair dark, Eyes blue, and whole appearance imposing.

"After the lapse of more than thirty years, I again had the privilege of meeting this friend of my youth, at the house of his sister in Chillicothe. He was now a valetudinarian, travelling in search of health. Years and disease had wrought a great change in his External appearance, but he still was the same cheerful, companionable man as in former days. Possessing an inexhaustible fund of valuable information, his conversation was uniformily interesting and Edifying. I could not, however, divest myself from the conviction that he must soon pass from the church in which he had labored on Earth, to the church triumphant in Heaven. The probable proximity of this change being adverted to in one of our conversations, although not surprised, I was rejoiced to find that that saving faith in Christ which he had so long recommended to others, was now his support. He spoke calmly of death, saying, that, in his case, it was an event rather to be desired than otherwise."

Dr. Doddridge being afflicted with asthma, & long under the impression that the Effluvia arising from the combustion of bituminous coal greatly aggravated his sufferings, resolved to test the hygenic Effect of a sojourn of one winter

[p. 33[12]]

in an atmosphere free from this, to him, deleterious matter. But the Experiment failing to result beneficially, & despairing of any favorable change in regard to his health, in the Spring he returned to his home in Virginia, there to await the welcome summons that should release him from suffering and from Earth.

He lingered some months after his return, without Experiencing any great increase of physical suffering, but from his knowledge of the human system, was well aware that the time of his departure was could not be far distant. During this period, he spoke of death with great composure. Renouncing all dependance save in the merits of his Savior, he felt no fear, but seemed anxious to depart.

His protracted sufferings terminated at his residence in Wellsburg, Brooke County, Virginia, on the 9th day of November, A.D. 1826, in the 57th year of his age.

Of the twelve children of Dr. Doddridge, four preceded him to the spirit land: three sons, and one daughter. His wife & four others have since joined him there, viz. Charles Hammond his youngest son died in Chillicothe in 1834, aged 18; Harriet T., wife of Maj. Wm. Duval, died at Fort Smith, Arks., in 1841; Mary D., wife

[p. 33[13]]
of B. F. Brannan, of Cincinnati, died in 1857; & Philip Bukey, his Eldest child, died in Columbus, Ohio, in 1860. Of the cheerful group which once surrounded his humble hearth, but four remain: one son, & three daughters.

[p. 34]
Early history of Greenbriar County, Virginia (Col. John Stuart's narrative)

About the year 1749 a person who was a citizen of the county of fredrick and subject to lunacy when under such paroxism usually made excursions into the wilderness and in his rambles westwardly fell in on the waters of Greenbriar river. The country at that day was little known to the inhabitants of the then colonies that lay upon the western waters being claimed by the Ten who had commenced settlements on the Ohio, and claimed all the country west of the Allegheny mountains. This person being surprised to find waters running a different course from any he had before known returned with the intelligence of his discovery which abounded with game this excited the enterprse of other when ② two men from new England of the name of Jacob Martin and Stephen Sewell took up a residence on Green Briar river but not agreeing they seperated and Sewell for peace sake quit the cabin and made his abode in a large hollow tree in this situation they were found by the late General Andrew Lewis near 1751. Mr. Lewis being appointed agent for the Green Briar Company who had obtained an order of council from the Executive of Colony of Va. for a grant of 100.00 acres of land lying on the waters of Green Briar did this year commence his surveying to complete the complement of the land granted as aforesaid: and finding Martin and Sewell in the neibourhood of each other enqured what could induce them to live separate so a wilderness far from the habitations of any other human being. They informed him that a difference of sentiment occasioned their seperation and that since they had enjoyed Greater comfort and a better understanding for Sewell told him that Esach morning when they arose Martin arose and came out of his great house

[p. 34²]
Saying good morning Mr. Sewell good morning Mr. Martin so that a good understanding prevailed at the present, but it seems did not last. For Sewell removed about 40

miles farther west to a creek which still bears his name where the indians found him and killed him. Previous to the year 1755 Mr. Lewis had completed surveys under the order of council to the amount of 50.000 Acres when the war commencing between England and France nothing farther was done on behalf of the grantees before 1761 when his majestys proclamation issued commanding all his subjects in the bounds of the colony of Virgina who had made settlements on the Western waters to remove from the same as the land were claimed by the Indians and policy required that a good understanding should be preserved with them to prevent hostilities on their part and the order of council was never carried in effect as his Majesty had never given consent to confirm it. At the commencement of the revolution when the State of Va. assumed an Independ... and held a convention in 1776 some effort was made to have the order of council established under the new order of things then taking place but it was not confirmed and commissioners were appointed in 1777 to grant to each individual who had mad settlement on the western Waters in this state a settlement ... for 400 acres ... acres more if they ch... to accept it and so much could be found exclusive of prior claims and on the following year (1778) green briar was seperated from Botetourt County and the new county took its name from the river so named by old Col John Lewis one of the original grantees under the order of council who in company with his son Andrew explored the country in 1751 entangled himself in a bunch of green briars ...

[p. 34³]
the river bank and declared he would ever afterward call that river Greenbriar. After peace was confirmed be-

tween England and France in the year 1761 the indians commenced hostilities in 1763 and all the inhabitants then residing in Greenbriar were totally surprised and cut off. The chief settlement was upon muddy Creek, a company of indians consisting of upwards of 60 under the mask of friendship introduced themselves into their houses and every civility was offered them by the people in providing every thing for their entertainment when on a sudden they killed all the men and made the women prisoners with their children thence they passed over into the Levels where some families were collected at the house of Archibald Clindennen where the Honble. Ballard Smith now resides in all about 60 persons. There the indians were entertained as at muddy Creek in the most hospitable manner, and Clendennen having just arrived from a hunt with 3 fat elks they were plentifully feasted.

In the mean time an old woman with a sore leg was shewing her distress to an indian and desiring to know if he could administer to her relief when he instantly killed her and nearly all the men in the house making prisoners of the rest women and children and here a scene of great cruelty took place amongst which a negro woman at a spring killed her own child who was running after crying and endeavouring to escape. Mrs. Clendennen did not fail to abuse the indians calling them cowards and other terms of reproach even when the tomahawk was drawn over her head and the scalp of her husband lashed about her jaws. The next day in crossing Keeneys Knob the prisoners being all in the center and the indians in the front and rear she gave her infant child to a woman to carry and she slipped into a thicket and made her escape. The cries of the child made the Indians enquire for the mother who was missing one of

[p. 34⁴]
said he would soon bring the cow to her calf and taking the child by the heels beat its brains out against a tree. She told me she returned that night to her own house and covered her husbands corps with rails it being a distance of 10 miles over mountains and through woods she then went into the cornfield when great fear came upon her and she imagined she saw a man standing within a few steps of her. The indians continued the war untill 1764 and committed much depredation upon our frontier inhabitants and making excursions as far as within a few miles of Stanton.

An end however was put to the war in the fall of that year by the advance of an army under the command of Col. Boquett a British officer who marched from fort Pitt and aided by several companies of Militia from Augusta Co. and other places who I believe either Volunteered or were such companies as government had ordered on the frontier to protect the settlements during the war. Col. Bouquett held a treaty with the Indians somewhere about Muskingum and many prisoners were delivered up and returned to their friends and peace concluded which continued till 1774 in the spring of which year Gen. Lewis represented the County of Botetourt in the assembly & his brother Col. Charles Lewis represented the county of Augusta. In the Month of may or April during the sitting of the assembly in Williamsburgh Government recd. intelligence of the Hostile intentions of the indians who had fallen on the traders of the nation and put them all to death and were making other arrangements for war. Gen. Lewis and his brother charles sent express immediately to the frontier requesting them to put themselves in a posture of immediate defence they had each the command of the Militia in their respective counties at the time and I was ordered by Gen. Lewis to send out some scouts to watch the warrior paths beyond the settlement in Greenbriar as our new settlements had only begun to recommence in 1769. We were few in number and not in a condition to oppose any considerable force succour was promised as soon as they would arrive from the Assembly. In the meantime, arrangements were made to carry on an expedition

[p. 34[5]]
against the shawanes as soon as possible with the Earl of Donnore who was the Governor of Va. In the course of that summer the Indians came up the Kenhawa and killed Walter Kelly, who had begun a settlement about 12 miles below the falls. At the time they made the attack Col. John Fields of Colpepper was at Kellys and about to make some surveys on military claims & otherwise he had with him several of his neighbours and 1 or 2 negroes. I had sent express for them to remove immediately as I apprehended from the intelligence I had received that they were in imminent danger. Kelly who was I believe a fugitive from the upper settlements of South Carolina and of a bold and Intrepid disposition recd. my intelligence with caution and sent off his family and stock for green-briar with his brother a young man of equally suspicious character. But Fields trusting more to his own consequence and knowledge of facts endeavoured to persuade Kelly there could be no danger as nothing of the kind had been before heard of and our green-briar intelligence not to be relied on. The evening Kelly had dismissed his family and brother and before they were out of hearing of the guns the Indians came upon Kelly and Fields who were drawing Leather from a tan trough some distance from their cabin and fired upon

them and Kelly was killed upon the spot & Fields ran to the cabin where their guns were standing all unloaded he picked up one but reccollecting they were not charged he ran out of the house into a cornfield a few steps from the door and left his negro girl and scotch girl crying at the door the boy was killed and the girl carried off. Fields made his escape but never seen an Indian.

  Kelly's brother informed me he heard the guns soon after he had left the house and I prepared to go and see the consequence. I raised 15 or twenty men and had command our march to the Kenhawa about 10 miles when I met Colo. Fields naked all but his shirt his limbs greviously lacerated with briars and brush and his body worn down with fatiuge and cold having run in that condition from the Kenhawa upwards of 80 miles through the woods, he was then I guess about 50 years old ... and robust constitution, he was afterward killed at the battle on the 10 of october following at point pleasant. A kind of fatality seemed to follow the family of the Kellys, for the Indians came to greenbriar about 3 weeks afterwards and killed young Kelly and took his brothers daughter prisoner. About this time the dispute between the British Government &

[p. 34[6]]
and the then colonies on account of the duty laid upon tea imported to this country ran high and much suspicion was entertained that the indians were urged by British agents to commence hostility and kill the traders however that might be a plan of expedition was concerted between the ear of Donmore before they left Williamsburgh and Genl. Lewis was to take command of the southern Division & his lordship in person was to command the northern. The troops were to be raised of volunteer Militia or otherwise

by Drafts those under Lewis to be raised in the counties of Augusta Botetourt and other counties adjacent below the blue ridge; those under the Governor from the counties of fredrick, shanandoah and the settlements extending fort Pitt. Colo. Charles Lewis was to have the command of the Augusta Volunteers, and Colo. Wm. Fleming the command of the command of the Botetourt Volunteers under Gen. Lewis, these troops assembled in Greenbriar at camp union where Lewisburgh now stands, about the 1st of September 1774 amounting in all to about 1100 men and commenced their march from there about the 11th of the same month. The captains commanding the Augusta volunteer companies were Capt. George Mathews Capt. Alexander McClenachan Capt. John Dickinson Capt. John Lewis Capt. Benjn. Harrison Capt. Wm. Hunt Capt. Joseph Hains & Capt. Saml. Wilson. Those commanding the Botetourt companies were Capt. Mathew Arbuckle Capt. John Murrey Capt. John Lewis Capt. Thos. Rowland Capt. Robert McClenachan Capt. James Ward and Capt. John Stewart from camp Union no track or way was made to the mouth of the great Kenawha a distance of 160 miles and the way very mountainous. In this route our principal pilot was Capt. Mathew Arbuckle. Our bread stuff was packed upon horses and droves of cattle furnished our meat of which we had a plentiful supply as pack horses and droves of cattle came in succession after us. Our way was exceeding rugged and bad but we went on expeditiously under every impediment until we arrived at point pleasant the mouth of the great Kenhawa about the first of October where we ex-

[p. 34[7]]
pected the Earl of Dunmore with his troops to meet. He was to have come down the Ohio as previouly agreed on

between the commanders. In this expectation we were exceedingly disappointed as the Earl had pursued a different rout and taken his march from Fort Pitt by land towards the Shawnee Towns. Genl. Lewis finding himself disappointed of meeting the Governor's troops at Point Pleasant dispatched some scouts by land up the river to Fort Pitt to know the cause of the disapointment and our army remained encamped to await their return. Before we marched from camp Union, we were joined by Colo. John Fields with a company of men from Culpepper and Capt. Thomas Buford with a company from Bedford County also two companies under the command of Evan Shelby and capt. Herbert from Holstein. These troops were to compose a division to be commanded by Col. William Christian who was at that time assembling more men in that quarter with a view of following us to the mouth of the Kenhawa where we were all to assemble and proceed from thence to the Shawnee Towns. The last mentioned companies compleated an army at camp Union amounting to Eleven hundred men.

  During the time our scouts were going express up the river to Fort Pitt the Governor had dispatched three men lately traders among the indians down the river express to Genl. Lewis informing him of his new plan and the rout he was about to pursue with instructions to Genl. Lewis to pursue his march to the Shawnee Towns wher he expected to assemble with us.

[p. 34[8]]
What calculations he might have made for delays or disappointments that would occasionally happen to two armies in so long a march thro' a trackless wilderness I cannot guess or how he could supose they would meet at a conjuncture so critical as the occasion required was

never known to any one. The Governors express arrived at our encampment on Sunday the 9th of October and on that day it was my duty to command the guard. One of the men of the name of McCollach with whom I had made some acquaintance in Philadelphia in 1776 at the Indian Queen where we both happened to lodge. This supposing I might be in <u>Lewis's</u> army inquired and was told I was then on guard he made it his business to visit me and renew our acquaintance. In the conversation I had with him he told me he had recently left the Shawnee Towns and repaired to the Governor's camp. I was desirous to know his opinion of our success and whether he thought the Indians would be so presumptuous as to dispute with force of arms against a force as superiour as ours. "Aye said they will give you grinders and that before long". This he repeated over and over again that we should get grinders very soon. I believe he left the camp that evening. Two young men set out early the next morning to take a hunt for deer and happened to ramble two or three miles up the river above our camp. Unexpectedly they came on the camp of the Indians who were just rising and preparing for battle. They discovered by the indians and fired on one of them was killed the other reached our

[p. 34⁹]
camp just before sunrise. It sloped just before my tent and I discovered as I lay a number of men collecting around him I jumped up and as I app... him I heard him declare he saw above fair acree of ground covered with Indians as thick as one could stand by the side of another.

<u>Genl. Lewis</u> immediately ordered a detachment of the Botetourt troops under <u>Col. Fleming</u> and another of August troops under <u>Colo. Charles Lewis</u>. These troops

were taken from the companies of the eldest Captains. The junior captains (of whom I was one) were ordered to stay in Camp as a reserve. The marched only in two lines and met the indians in the same order about four hundred yards from the camp. The indians made the first fire and killed both the souts a little distance in front of the two lines. Just as the sun was rising a very heavy fire commenced. Col. Lewis was mortally wounded but walked into camp and died in his own tent Saying with his last breath that he had sent one Indian to eternity before him.

During the life of Col. Lewis it was his lot to have frequent skirmishes with the indians in which he was always successful had gained much applause for his intrepidity and was greatly beloved by his troops. Col. Fleming was wounded and our men had given way some distance before a reinforcment got out of camp to their aid when Indians in their turn had to retreat untill they formed a line behind logs and trees reaching from the bank of the Ohio to the bank of the Kenkawa and kept up their fire untill sun down.

[p. 34[10]]
They were exceedingly active in concealing their dead. In the midst of the batle I saw a young draw out three of them whose bodies werre cavered by leaves by the side of a large log.

Col. Christian reached us with his troops about Eleven Oclock the night after the battle. In the morning he marched his men over the battle ground and found 21 dead bodies of the enemy 12 more were afterwards found in a concealed place. The indians acknowleged that during the battle they had thrown a considerable number of their dead into the river.

The indians were commanded by the Cornstalk

warrior who displayed much generalship in his plans of attack and retreat.

On our side we had 75 men killed and 14 wounded. Amongst our killed were Cols. Lewis and Felds Captains Buford Murray Ward, Wilson McClenachan Lieutenants Allen Goldsby Dillen and some other subaltern officers.

Colo. Fields I believe had raised his company under no particular instructions and seemed from the time he joined the army at camp Union to assume a kind of independance not subject to the contrant of others. This claim might have originated in a belief that a former station in some military station in which he had been engaged entitled him to a rank that ought not to subject him to lne controul under our volunteer commanders. He therefore took a different rout and on the third day after our departure from camp Union two of his men of the names of Coward and Clay who had left the company to look for deer fell in with two Indian on the waters of the little meadows and as Clay passed round

[p. 34[11]]
the end of a lying tree one of the indians who was concealed under its roots killed him and coming up to him was killed by Coward who was distant about one hundred yards from them. The other Indian escaped and passed some of our scouts without arms.

A bundle of ropes which was found wher Clay was killed manifested their design to steal horses. Col. Fields never separated from us after this.

After the battle we had many accounts of the number of Indians who attacked us. Some asserted that there more than a Thousand. Some assumed that their number did not exceed Four Hundred. The correct number I believe was never ascertained by us but it is certain they were combined of different tribes Shawnees Windots and Delawares. Of the former no doubt the whole strength of the nation was engaged in the battle.

On the evening before the battle when they were about to cross the river as we were enformed by good authority the Cornstalk proposed to the Indians if they were willing he would approch our camp and offer terms of peace to us but but they would not agree to the proposal. And it was reported that during the battle he killed one of his own men for making a precipitate and cowardly retreat. I could hear him the whole day speaking to his troops in a loud voice and one of my men who had been a prisoner among the Indians told me that what he was vociferating was "Be strong be strong".

The Indians passed the river in the night and made the best of their way to their Towns on the Scioto.

After burying our dead Gen. Lewis

[p. 34[12]]
ordered intrenchments to be made across the point from the Ohio to the Kenhawa to secure the wounded under an officer with a number of men adequate for their safety While he pursued his march across the Ohio for the Shawnee Towns. In this command he had to encounter difficulties that none can judge of who have never experienced similar difficuties. To preserve order and discipline over an army of volunteers who had no knoledge of the use of discipline or the necessity of order in an enemy's country well skilled in their own mode of warfare. It is well known that the youth of our country previous to that time had been raised in times of peace and totally unacquainted with military operations of any kind this together with a high notion of self independence and

equality of condition rendered the service difficult and disagreeable to the commander who was by nature of a lofty and high military spirit and who had seen much Service under Genl. Braddock and other military commanders and at the time Genl. Washington was appointed by Gov. Gooch to erect a fort at the little meadows in the year 1753 to prevent the incursions of the French who were extending their claims from Fort Pitt up the Monongahela and its waters Genl. Lewis and Capt. Peter Flag were appointed his captains and during the time they were employed in erecting the garrison received the attack made on them by a party of French sent out from fort Duquesne that purpose on account of an unfortunate which took place soon after they had arrived at the little Meadows.

A French gentleman of the name of

[p. 34[13]]
Junenville who with his party was making some surveys not far from Major Washingtons encampment and he ordered Capt. Hogg to go and examine him as to his authority for making such an encroachment on the British claims and Settlements. Capt. Hogg discovered Junenville's encampment which he approached in the night time and contrary to his orders or the instructions of Major Washington he fired upon Junenville without giving any previous notice and killed him and the French in order to retaliate sent out a party to attack Washington, they were discovered when about a mile from the encampment & soon appeared before it and commenced firing as they approached it. Our people had made some entrenchments and from which they returned the fire and in this engagement Gen. Lewis recd. two wounds the French soon cried out for a parley and the firing on both sides ceased and

the parties intermixed indiscriminately and articles of a capitulation were drawn up by the French which Major Washington signed and acknowledged. He was then a very young man and unacquainted with the French Language and it seems in that capitulation Major Washington acknowledged the murder of Junenville this was sent to Europe & published and Hostilities soon commenced between the two rival nations England and France and the foundation of the war of 1755 was cheifly grounded on this quarrel. I have seen Bissels account of these transactions in his history of England which differs something from this but I have narrated the facts as I heard them from Genl. Lewis and I have no doubt of their truth. The French had brough in their party a number of Indians which gave them a great superiority in point of number and an accident occurred during the intermixture of the parties which migh have been fatal to washington and all his men had not Genl. Lewis with great presence of mind prevented it. An Irish Soldier walking in the crowd with his musket seeing an Indian near him presented his musket, swearing in the language of his country he would send the Yellow Son of a Bitch to Hell. Gen. Lewis was limping near him with his wounded leg and with his hand struck the muzzle of the gun into the air and saved the Indian and perhaps of many others had the Irishmans

[p. 34[14]]
intention taken effect.

  When the war in 1755 began Col. Washington was appointed commander of the first regiment was raised in Virginia and Genl. Lewis major and was afterwards on command with the noted Major Grant of the British army. By order of Genl. Forbes to reconnoitre the vicinty of the French fort Du Quesne and approaching the garrison without being discovered Grant began to entertain the opinion that he could surprize the garrison and disappoint his Genl. of the honour of its conquest.

Against this unjustifiable attempt Majr. Lewis in vain remonstrated but Grant unwilling to share the honour of so great an enterprise ordered Lewis and his party to stay back with their baggage whilst he advanced with his highlanders to the assault. He began by beating the drums of on Grants hill about day-light in the morning. Fifteen hundred indians were at that time lying on the western bank of the Alegheny opposite the fort. The sound of war so near them so sudden and so unexpected soon roused them to arms and Grant and his Scotchmen were instantly surrounded and the work of death went on rapidly in a manner quite novel to Highlanders who in all their European wars had never seen mens heads shaved before.

Lewis soon discovered by a retreating fire that Grant was in a bad situation. He advanced with his corps of two hundred men and falling on the rear of the Indians made a way for Grant and some of his men to escape but Lewis's party was also defeated and himself taken prisoner. The Indians were desirous of puting him to death and the French with

[p. 34[15]]

difficulty prevented them. They striped him of all his clothes but his shirt before he was taken into the garrison. An elderly Indian seized the shirt but he resisted with the tomahack over his head untill a French officer by signs requested him to deliver it to the Indian. This officer took him naked into his room and furnshed him with a complete suit. Grant had made his escape from the field of battle and with a party of Seven or Eight soldiers had wandered all night in the woods and in the morning returned to the garrison and surrendered themselves prisoners to the Indians who carried them into the fort. Majr. Grants life was saved by the French but the Indians brought the soldiers to the room door where Majr. Lewis was his benefactor refused to let them come in and they killed all the men at the door.

The French expecting the main army under Genl. Forbes would soon arrive and the fort and garrison being considered not in a state capable of making blew up the fort and retreated to Quebeck with all the prisoners where they were confined until a cartel took place when they were exchanged.

It has been said that Majr. Grant has since figured in the british Parliament but during the time of his captivity he was detected in an act of the basest duplicity. The letters of the british officers were not suffered to be sealed untill they were inspected by a French officer discovered that in Majr. Grants communication to Genl. Forbes he had represented the whol disgrace of their defeat to the misconduct of Majr. Lewis and his provincial troops.

[p. 34[16]]
The officer immediately carried the letter to Majr. Lewis and shewed it to him. Lewis indignant at such a scandalous and unjust representation accused Grant of his duplicity in the presence of the French officers and challenged him but Grant prudently declined the combat after receiving the grossest insults by spiting in his face and degrading language.

Genl. Lewis was in person upwards of Six feet high of uncommon strength and agility and his form the most exact symmetry I ever beheld in any human being. He had a stern and invincible countenance was of a distant and reserved deportment which rendered his presence more awful than engaging and when he was at fort Stanwick in the province of New York in the year 1768 a commissioner with Dr. Thos. Walker to hold a treaty on behalf of the colony of Virginia with the six nations of indians together with commissioners from Pensylvania and N York it was remarked by the Governor of New York "that the earth seemed to tremble under him as he waked along. His independent spirit despised popularity which never rendered him more than his superior merits extorted.

Such a character was not calculated to gain much applause from commanding an army of volunteers without discipline, experience or gratitude and many took umbrage because they were compelled to do their duty.

When Congress made their first appointments of general officers to prosecute the war in defence of our liberties his great modesty recommended Genl. Lewis in preference to himself, but one of his colleagues from Virginia observed that Genl. Lewis's popularity had suffered much from the declamation of some of his troops

[p. 34[17]]
on the late expidition against the Indians and that at that juncture it would be impolitic to make the appointment. He was however afterwards appointed a Brigadier General and took the command of the troops at Norfolk after Lord Dunmore had made his escape from Williamsburgh on board a british ship of war lying off Norfolk. The vessel drew up and commenced a fire on the Fort but Genl. Lewis from a battery compelled his Lordship to depart and I believe he never afterwards set his foot on American ground and this ended the military career of Genl. Lewis. Congress having appointed Genl. Stevens and

some others as Majr. Genls. gave him some offence as he had been their superor in former services and having accepted his office of Brgadier at the solicitation of Genl. Washington he wrote the Genl. notice of his intention to resign. Genl. Washington however pressed him to hold his command and assured him that justice would be done him as it respected his rank but he was growing old and his ardour for military fame much abated and being seized with a fever resigned his commission to return home in the year 1780 and died on his way in Bedford County about 40 miles from on Roanoake in Bottetourt County lamented by all who knew his many meretorious services and superior qualities.

I have been told there is a book extant under the title of Smith's travels in America which was wrote on England in which the author asserts that he was in the expedition in 1774 and that he joined the Augusta troops in Staunton. He gives a description of Mr. Samn. Mathews tavern and family who kept the most noted publick house in Town and of our march from camp Union and the particulars of the battle and the death of Col. Lewis who was killed

[p. 35]
in the engagement.

Col. John Stuart's Narrative.

The foregoing Narrative I found in a Manuscript book containing the first draft of Doddridge's Notes and until a day or two ago had escaped my notice. It may be the continuation of the one of which I sent you a few pages many years ago, the whole of which, I remember you expressed a strong desire to have; I therefore send it, altho' I doubt whether it will be of any use to you, as the principal facts contained in it are already matters of history.

N. D.

[p. 36]

Narrative of John Bingeman

This man high up the south fork of the South branch. The time 1763.

The Indian came into the house in the in the house. One came in first and attepted to shoot him but shot over him and shot his wife in one of her breasts. B. jumped up, caught his rifle and shot the indian down. Four more more came in succession whom he knoucked down as fast as they came. The sixth, came while B. was killing the fifth, with his tomahark in his hand, raised it and would have killed him but for a young woman who by this time had jumped out of bed: she caught the Indian in her arms and held him fast. She fall back, and held him on her as she laying on her back still holding on to him as she lay on her back while B. killed him with a tomahawk. The Seventh Indian ran off. B. bough up one of the Indians guns and shot at him but missed him. His wife recovered of her wound.

Benjeman was made a captain. He now made a scout to the westward both ... not the captains in front both shot and missed. B in turing round fell the Indian made at him throwed his tomahawk and missed him. B. caught the tomahawk throwd at the Indian missed while the Indian was stooping to pick up the tomahawk B struck him in side knocked him down and then caught up the tomahawk. B ... defeated the Indians.

Letters of a "Russian Spy"

Russian Spy

Dear Galitzer

It is now a long time since you have heard from me but you are not to suppose on that account that I have forgotten either yourself or my my business in this New World for I do assure you that both the one and the other have been constantly present to my mind.

Should you ask me "What I have been about?" My answer would be that I have been an attentive observer of men and things in this country with a view the letter to fulfill my mission here. You my dear friend need not complain of the interruption of our intercourse. It will result to your own advantage and I hope to many others as well as yourself.

A journalist to be correct and useful in his descriptions of countries and views of the manners and custom of society requires time and much labour.

Facts ought to be recorded on the spot. Theoretic deductions from them ought to be slowly and cautiously made. Many customs which appear strange and even absurd at first sight appear quite otherwise when taken in connection with the general system of manners to which they belong. We should have patience therefore to view the whole portrait before we attempt to decide on any part of it.

Few travellers are competent to the task of adding much to the science of the world by them researched. Some are deficient in science. Others are to lazy. A still greater number are too much by prejudce to be impartial. With them the standards of all that is good great and polite in human nature is to be found exclusively in the manner and customs of their own nation. The result is that they judge unfavourably of almost everything they see.

Scarcely any journalist pays a proper attention to the ... of those foreign countries and customs which they attempt to describe. I have scarcely read a book of travels with which I was satified, and mainly on this account. When I finished the book I regretted that I did not know more of every subject it contained than the author thought proper to tell me. Another class invalidate their credibility by mixing too much of the romantic with their narrations.

With my talents for this as well as other kind of composition you my friend are well acquainted. Partiality for my native county God knows, is not likely to be my fault for what has my country been to me? A region of sorrow and affliction. My life has been laborious and I trust useful but marked at every step with misfortune. In the midst of surrounding abundance I have been doomed to all the pains and penalties of chill penurey. Amongst numbers possessed of wealth or competence and whose blood runs in my veins I have been suffered to want bread. After administering to the wants and health of others then in affliction myself I have not found a Good Samaritan to pour the oil and wine of consolation into my wounds but have left to grapple with sickness and want as I could.

There seems to be a strange fatality in the affairs of men. Some men of the greatest and most useful talents faithfully exerted for publick and private good have been throughout the unoffending victims of poverty and incessant persecution yet no one can tell for what reason. Every thing considered as due from them to his fellow men yet little sense of obligation to remunerate their services is felt by any on whom they confers even the most important services. Thus they live and die neglected and their value to society is never known or acknowledged till they drop into the grave. Posthumous praise is all they inherit from the world. Such for the most part have been the real benefactors of mankind.

On the other hand we have seen many men on whom an unmeritted amount of patronage has been conferred. They were honoured credited carrossed paid in advance. The idols of the country but for what reason no one can tell. So capricious is fortune with regard to the living. This latter class often fail of fulfilling their obligations to society and of course leave society to regret the loss of patronage so prematurely and improperly bestowed.

The fate of the former class has been mine. The result is that I am under no obligation of duty to my country or to my community of people. I am free to go where I please and spend my time in any way I may judge proper. May from the cold neglect and downright injustice bestowed on me would have become downright misanthropist committed suicide or taken in robbery murders and arsons. I have done none of those things on the contrary I have by every means in my power expressed the spirit of revenge by asscribing my untoward fatality to circumstances. He who ever so faithfully excercises a literary profession the fees of which are honorary among an unenlightened and avaricious people need never expect a reward for his services. In proportion to the number of his good deeds he is sure to make enemies as ingratitude is the readiest change for paying off obligations of this sort. Thus at liberty to dispose of myself as I choose and free from prejudice and partialities I think myself well qualified to execute the work in which I am engaged. Viewing makind thro' no inverted or dusky medium I can see and describe them as they really are.

Adieu

[p. 38]
Dear Galitzer

It must have occurred to you from reading and observation that the human passions the instruments of so much moral good and evil may be subdued either by the iron hand of despotism or by the influence of superstition but that in free governments like that of this country those powerful means by which they are repressed in other countries so as to reduce the man to mere obedienct machine in the hands of others do not exist here.

An American is free. He is Lord of the soil which he cultivates and he with his compeers possess the sovereignty of the country and he has the choice of his own religion or if such be his wish he may have none at all. To the suffrages the male population of the country the legislators the governors of the differents States and even the President himself owe their devotion. The period for which they are elected is but short. If their conduct while in office does not give satisfaction they are sure not to be re-elected but dismissed with disgrace. This is the ostracism of this country and a severe one it is.

My good friend if despotism has its gloom liberty has its tempest. Here every passion exists in full vigour and every object of human ambition has its full effect. Every one pursues any course of life he chooses and does whatever is is right in his own eyes.

You will naturally enquire in what way the strong passions of these republicans find an outlet? Surely you will say there must be some barriers against which those turbulent waves of passion and ambition may dash and dissipate their violence.

There are barriers to the strong passion and ambition of these people which have the effect of dissipating and rendering them harmless. I will proceed to state them as they present themselves to my mind.

You will be surprized when I inform you that the religion of this country serves as an outlet for an immense amount of ambition. Yet such is the fact. Here reformation upon reformation has taken place to an astonishing extent. The followers of Luther are cleft into several societies. Those of Calvin are still more divided. The pulpit here is the theatre for oratory disputation satire crimination and the full display of all those violent passions which have for their object the making of proselytes from all other communities.

These pages of the R. Spy are Just merely to give you an idea of the character of the latters.

[p. 39]
Capture of members of the Doddridge family

The particulars of the following narrative of the murder of a member of the family of Philip Doddridge Sen. and the capture of three of his children by a party of Wyandotts, in 1778, were derived from two of his nieces, Mrs. Ellen D. Brown, late of Wellsburg, Virginia, and Mrs. Ruth Carson, late of Ross Ct. Ohio.

Philip Doddridge sen. and his brother John emigrated from their native State, Maryland, in 1770. The latter stopped in Pennsylvania, but the former continued westward until he reached the mouth of Dunkard Creek, a tributary of the West Branch of the Monongahela, where he made a settlement. At the time the Indians visited his domicile, he had a comfortable cabin and a tolerably well improved farm.

His household consisted of a wife, four young children, his wife's father, mother and a nephew, a lad of twelve years.

Early one morning in the month of May, 1778, Mr. Doddridge went to work in one of his fields, some distance from his home, his wife also being absent; She having taken her infant and gone to the house of a friend to do some weaving for her family.

[p. 39[2]]
Their three little girls, between the ages of two and seven years, were left in the care of their grand-parents and the lad above mentioned.

While he was amusing the children at the base of a high bank of the Creek on which they lived, he espied in the distance a party of Indians approaching the house, which they, without perceiving him, entered, tomahawked and scalped the aged grandfather, took from the cabin such articles as they fancied, and then set it on fire, leaving the body of the murdered man to be consumed with it. The nephew well aware that if he remained with his little charge, he could not protect them, and would himself be killed or captured, fled by a circuitous path to the place where his uncle was at work, and informed him of what was transpiring at home. They both saw the flames of the burning building and the savages amusing themselves by ripping open the feather beds and throwing their contents high in the air. Having finished their work at the cabin, the deeply afflicted father was compelled to remain where he was and see the Indians bearing off into the forest his three little girls and their aged grandmother without the power to afford them the slightest relief.

Soon after this sad catastrophe, Philip,

[p. 39³]
with his wife and remaining child, left the vicinity of the Monongahela, and went to the house of his brother John Doddridge, who had in 1773, removed from Bedford County, Pa. to the western part of Washington Ct. in the same State, locating but a short distance from the present village of West Middletown. Philip subsequently purchased from his brother in law, Captain Samuel Teter, a farm near his brother's, on which he resided till about 1818, when he removed with his family, then consisting of one son, John, and five daughters, to the State of Indiana, himself performing the whole journey on foot, for altho' possessing an abundance of this world's goods, he was never known to ride on horseback or in a carriage. He was one of the early friends and supporters of Methodism in the Western Country, and so exemplary was his life, that wherever he was known, his influence was felt.

The precise fate of the aged grandmother was never ascertained, but very many years after the capture of their children, the parents learned that they had been taken to Detroit, where the eldest girl was sold to a French officer, who took her to France, educated and afterwards married her. The second one died, and the third, being reared with the children of her tawny captor, became as one of them, married a chief, and altho' herself well acquainted with her parentage, so strong was her attachment to the mode of life in which she had been brought up that she carefully concealed her relationship to her family.

The late Philip Doddridge, Esq., of Wellsburg, Va., told the writer that this woman had often been at his house with other Indians who came into Virginia

[p. 39⁴]
to dispose of baskets, moccasons and other articles of their own manufacture. After seing and conversing with her several times, he recognized her resemblance to her family, and made some enquiries respecting her history, telling her that he was her cousin, and offering to take her to see another of her cousins, Rev. Dr. J. Doddridge. He said she looked alarmed and displeased, ceased to converse, left his house, and never after, to his knowledge, returned to that part of the Country.

We have been informed that the late Rev. James B. Finley, of Ohio, said that while he was a Missionary among the Wyandott Indians, he was well acquainted with this captive and her family, and that after the settlement of her parents in Indiana, they visited her and endeavored to prevail on her to return with them but without success. Whether this latter statement be correct or not, we are not able to say.   July 1861.

[p. 40]
An Elegy
on the death of Eliza M. Doddridge, who died January the 11th 1819, aged 15 years, by her Father, Rev. Dr. J. Doddridge.

My dear Eliza! Thou art gone,
Thou sweet, thou lovely, child!
Thy little span, has quickly run,
And all our hopes beguil'd.

Why hast thou thus impartial death,
Destroy'd so fair a prize?
Thy dart which laid her in the earth,
Makes thousands bleed besides!

Thy lovely form, thy polish'd mind,
To all thy friends are lost.
Thy tender heart, and taste refin'd,
Are laid with thee in dust.

For thee no more thy garden flowers
Shall shed their rich perfume,
For thee no more thy garden bowers
Shall give their shade at noon.

No more thy song, no more thy lyre
Shall charm thy lov'd abode,
No more those eyes which sparkl'd fire
Shall beam on those she lov'd.

Thy deeds were good, thy faith correct,
And all thy thoughts were pure.
We lov'd thee much: can we regret
Thy God has lov'd thee more?

Why have I learn'd that all must part,
And bid the world farewell?
'Tis now I feel death's fatal dart,
And breathe his gloomy spell.

Again! again! The gush of grief,
Bursts from the heart in tears.
Again! again! I ask relief,
But find no confort near.

Let the companions of her youth,
Weep round her funeral pall!
Forget her not, tho' sunk in death,
For much she lov'd you all.

Thou shalt not leave me, No! my child!
My faith still claims thy cares,
Be thou my guardian angel mild,
In my declining years.

Well hast tho fled a world of pain.
Tho' sad thy parting knell,
So soon we all shall meet again,
We will not say — FAREWELL.

Wellsburg, Virginia,
1819.

[p. 41]

An Elegy

On the death of R. Reeves Doddridge, who died in Chillicothe, O. on the 9 of January, 1825: aged 11 years. By his Father, Rev. Dr. Joseph Doddridge, of Wellsburg, Va.

O! strike ye Angels, strike the lyre,
    And softly breathe your sweetest dirge,
O! welcome to your heavenly choir
    The little Saint you have in charge.
O! sound your harps, ye heavenly band,
    And ev'ry voice the hymn prolong;
The portal past, in Canaan's land,
    He joins you in your holy song.

Blest be the hand which led my child
    Into the sacred house of God;
The place with grace and mercy fill'd
    The house of Jesus' blest abode.
Blest be the Altar where he knelt,
    And pour'd out his soul in prayer;

Blest be the mercy which he felt,
    And wip'd away the falling tear.

He is not dead: nay! but he sleeps;
    His cold, and dark, but hallowed rest,
O'er which his friends will often weep,
    Is with his angel's presence blest.
Yet Death stood by, his dart half drawn;
    This little Saint is not your prey.
His angel said, "O! Death, begone."
    Then bow'd and kiss'd his soul away.

[p. 42]
Letter from Philip Doddridge to Benjamin Biggs

    Morgan Town August 10th 1796

Dr. Sir, I have undertaken a most damnable action in the District court together with Mr. Relfe on behalf of a certain Mr. Charles Donaldson at the Suit of the Commonwealth.

Mr. Chips is about to be Sent for the prisoner in Our county Goal may be indicted for A misdemeanor on his confession for having countenanced, after the fact, for aiding & abetting or countenancing in flight, or as a receiver of Stolen goods knowingly.

It is proposed and wishd here that he Should as soon as Law will permit be tried by an Examining Court and transmitted to the District Goal in order that his Testimony may be instantly be had to Justify proceedings Against his associates here in case Any of them Should be apprehended for without Any Evidence their apprending would only introduce their immediate discharge and render all further proceedings frustrated.

If he is not regularly committed he Ought to be, and a court call'd after five days.

If they apply to me as council I shall try the companies fund, or appear on the behalf of the Commonwealth against them.

I have the Honor to be yr. ...bl Serv
P. Doddridge
Benjamin Biggs Esq

Honl. Benjamin Biggs
Ohio County

[p. 43]
Letter from Philip Doddridge to Benjamin Biggs

Charles Town 4 December 1804

Dr. Sir. On acct. of a contact I have made at Lancaster I shall be much in want of money on the 1 March next & have every sum for collection I reasonably could. If it will be convenient to you at that time to pay me the Ballance between us without detriment to yourself it will much accomodate me & if so I will thank you to drop me a line at Richd. during the first week of January informing me whether you can or not, as it will enable me to know what arrangements otherwise to make on my return thro' Lancaster.

9 Apl 91	I believe the acct stands thus		
	your due Bill of Apl 1801		69.94
	cash paid by me on Mitcelfs Judgt. against you and Martin		14.24
9 Dec.	To cash at your house	2.00	
	To cash list at Wheeling		10.00
	Ditto at Moores		3.00
Aug. 6	To cash at J. Goodings	<u>8.00</u>	

```
                                107.18
        By Cash on acct. J. Harrison 13.00
        Ditto paid me to make up}
        the 14.24 paid Metcalf   }    1.24   14.24
                                      92.94
1804 Jany 13 By order on N.
        Lane for                     149.20
        By cash omitted 6 Apr   6.
        To cash same time                     9.10
        To Linsleys receipt for fees &
            gazette                          11.00
        To cash same day                      1.50
Feby. 7   Ditto                      18.00
        Ditto at I. Chaplines Store          20.00
March 7   To cash Wheeling           10.00
        To cash by Geo. Metcalf              20.00
March 7   To cash Wheeling           10.00
    11    To cash by Geo. Metcalf    20.00
May 2    paid J. Doddridge            5.00
    7    To cash by McKeever         20.00
        To cash by E. Dodᵍᵉ. to
            Short Creek                     20.00
        Ditto paid Mrs. Biggs                6.00
        Ditto paid by James Caldwell  2.50
                            155.20   236.04
                                     155.20
                                      80.84
```

There may be errors in this & if so they can be correct, & you'l understand I do not wish you to put yourself to an inconvenience.

      My comps. to Mrs. Biggs
           Yours Sincerely   P. Doddridge

Brooke ...
Dec. 8

Genl. Benjamin Biggs
West Liberty
Mail   Virginia

[p. 44]
Letter from Philip Doddridge to Benjamin Biggs

The debt is $2280, with interest 5.97 Intl. from 15 May 1818.

 The extent of $150 per annum will reduce debt and interest in $176 years you will be Safe in Selling for about that period.

 You are entitled to rents for the present year and those in possession must pay you. They had better take losses under you unless you can sell soon.

 Per the execution give a forthcoming bond.

 Next Monday I shall be at Court in Washington & will see whether the Bank will interfere or not, & will take from the Brices a conveyance to you.

    Yours
    P. Doddridge
    11 June 1818

Genl. Benjn. Biggs.

Memo
Gl. Biggs

[p. 45]
Invoices for cotton traded at Tuscaloosa Falls, Ala.

Invoice of 45 Bales Cotton Sold Peter A. Remsen by Mr. M. H. Galaspie May 27th 1820 Tuscaloosa falls as follows

```
#27. 225              Levi Robunload
 28. 236              255
 29. 212              251
 30. 208              260           Mr. Goode
 31. 228  ‡Browne    258           256}
    1109lb            255           267}
    2050              261           255}Beanes
    1828              248           247}
    2144              262           277}
    2209             2050 lb        270}
    2351                            1572}
   11751lb           Bias          256}Beanes
                                   1828 lb

                 Thomas Goode      246}
                                   273}
                                   256}
                                   253}‡Browne
                                   265}
                                   259}
Joseph Goode                       254}
    249}                           1806
    259}
    242}        Adam Fair   338   Keywood
    260}                   2144 lb
    250} ‡ Browne
    252}           Thomas Potter
    243}           8 bales Gin Weight
    256}                2351 lb Wattons
    258}
   2269 lb
  11751 lb          E E
   2300 at 13 lbs   $299.00
   9451 lb at 12%  1181.37½
```

$1480.37½   May 29th 1820
             E ꭰ
       Reepay in full
              M H Gillespie

Epicac
Angekoks
buckberry called
by early settlers on frontier See
bog-berry or cranberry
Service tree or mountain ash

Micajah Mayfield
May 1835

[p. 46]
Letter from Philip Doddridge to John C. Wright

Richmond   16 Dec 1828
Dear Sir
        I received yours of the 13th Inst for which I thank you.
        There was a Suit tried at the last Circuit court at Columbus, Bank U. States agt. Carneal & others & judgment given for the defendant. Benham Carswell and Fox were Counsel for Plff and Hammond and I for defendant.
        The Plffs took a writ of error, and I requested Col. Bond when he made out the record on the writ of error to make and Send me a copy as defendants Counsel as it would cost my client less to get it there than at Washington.
        The envelope you sent is that copy and the record you have must have been Sent to you at the request of the ... of the same to be handed to the Clerk of the Supreme

Court to be entered.

I will thank when you ... it to the Clerk to tell him to enter my appearance for the defendant in error. This done the case will possably be heard this winter.

No news here. We shall have, I fear, an any storm when our Convention ... Shall ...

Very Respectfuly
P. Doddridge

[Postmark] RICHd. Va.
 D C
Hon. John C. Wright
H. Rep.
Washington D. C.

P. Doddridge

[p. 47]
Obituary of Philip B. Doddridge

On Tuesday, the 11th of September [1860], the remains of our late fellow-citizen, Mr. Philip B. Doddridge, were consigned to their last resing place in Green Lawn Cemetery, accompanied by a large number of acquaintances and friends. The funeral services were at St. Paul's church, and were witnessed by a large and deeply affected assembly.

The funeral anthem was chanted by the choir, and after reading the lesson, the Rector proceeded to deliver a funeral discourse, dwelling on the solemn and affecting aspects of death, in its relations to this and the future world, and urging all present to be in readiness for the coming of the Bridegroom. He closed his remarks by the following reference to the character of the deceased:

Mr. Doddridge was blessed with pious parents, so that his religious training commenced in child hood. His father was a clergyman in the Episcopal church, and was eminently successful in introducing christianity into the south eastern portion of the State at an early day. In youth the conduct of Mr. D. was marked by great sobriety and decorum — he was temperate, moral and honest. When he grew to manhood he made a public profession of Christ, and connected himself with P. E. church, at Portsmouth, under the ministry of the Rev. Mr. Kellogg, more than forty years ago. From that time until the period of his death, he was an active, earnest and consistent christian, carrying his profession into all the duties and relations of life. He was a living illustration of the life and power of Godliness, in changing the heart, and renewing the nature and making us new creatures in Christ Jesus. He was a man of unbending integrity, and great decision of character. He formed his conclusions after mature reflection, and then he adhered to his convictions of duty and of right with unfaltering perseverance.

Mr. D. occupied various positions in the church, in all of them approving himself a workman that need not be ashamed. As vestryman, and warden, and Sunday school teacher, and Superintendent, he was worthy of all commendation. The last named office he has filled in this church for more than a year past with eminent success. He has here, and elsewhere, performed a noble work in this department of moral and religious instruction. Many of the young, through his labors, have been brought into the church, and will shine as stars in his crown of rejoicing in the kingdom of heaven forever.

Though ardently attached to the church of his choice, in its doctrines and ecclesiastical polity, Mr. Doddridge was no bigot. He recognized as genuine members of the household of faith all those who professed the name of Christ, and exhibited the spirit of Christ, wherever he found them. He always and every where breathed forth the sentiment of Jehonadab, the son of Rechab: "Is thy heart right, as my heart is with thine, if so give me thy hand."

Mr. D. was also an earnest friend and advocate of the temperance reformation. He had been connected with the movement from the beginning. He looked upon it as intimately related to the prosperity and welfare of the country. He regarded intemperance as the great curse of the age — as the foe of man, of the Bible, and of the church. Hence, he devoted time, and money, and influence to the removal of the evil. Those of you who have been united with him in this work of faith, and labor of love, and are here today as a testimonial of your high regard for your deceased brother, feel that you have lost a valuable co-laborer in the great work of drying up the streams of intemperance and vice in this city. I trust his mantle may fall on some one who will stand forth as a fearless advocate of the principles you are all laboring to establish.

I may say in few words that Mr. D. was a practical, experimental christian — a devoted friend of the church — a genuine philanthropist, with a heart always ready to respond to the calls of the needy — and an enterprising, public spirited citizen. He was a kind husband, and father, and neighbor, filling the various stations he occupied so as to deserve the commendation of "well done good and faithful servant." In his death this parish has lost one of its most useful members — the Sunday school an experienced and successful Superintendent — the friends of temperance and humanity a faithful co-laborer — his widow has lost a husband and protector — his grand children have lost a friend whose heart yearned to them with a father's affection — and this community has lost a valuable citizen. And while others are bereaved, I too have lost a friend to whom I could always go for sympathy and council, and upon whose judgment I placed the utmost confidence.

The death of Mr. Doddridge, like his life, exhibited the genuine christian. He endured his last sickness, of more than five weeks, with the most remarkable patience. Not a murmur escaped his lips. His condition for a time was not regarded as critical, but his disease eluded the skill of his physicians, and gradually his strength declined. I often spoke to him about his spiritual condition, and always received assurances of his unwavering trust in Christ. He stated that that at the beginning of his sickness, he had committed himself and all his interests into the hands of the Saviour; and he felt assured that he would keep what he had committed to him unto final salvation. He felt assured of his acceptance with God, and that whether he lived or died he was the Lord's. Thus he calmly waited until his change came, and without a cloud, or a doubt, he passed to his heavenly home.

"Servant of God, well done,
The battle's fought, the victory's won."

[p. 48]
Tutela, an Indian novel, by Joseph Doddridge
Unfinished

Had my father completed this sketch of Indian character, it would have been an interesting and valuable document. So far as it goes it will show you that the writer was a philosophist.

I send it merely for your perusal.

Chapter 1

The great water where the sun wakes up in the morning spread thro' the whole of the Indian nations with the rapidity of lightning. The Indians flocked from all quarters to see the strange beings.

Tutela with father was amongst the early visters of the Englishmen and Sir Walter Raleigh of Shore of the James's River. Young as he was when he saw the people and their ships and had heard the explosion and witnessed the effects of the balls of their artilery and musquetry he foresaw the downfall of his people. In the war which followed he distinguished himself as a young war chief but with the melancholy presentiment of the ultimate defeat of the Indian nations which accordingly took place. The country of his nativity was gradually taken possession of the whites part by purchase and partly by right of conquest.

The Indian of North America possesses a proud haughty sense of independence. He scorns the presence and rejects with disdain the clams of a superior. In all ancient history we meet with the master and the slave but the Indian knows nothing of slavery. Their prisoners were either executed or adopted into the families of such as had lost sons in the war. They were never doomed to slavery but after their adoption were as free as the rest of the nation to which they belonged.

The English who settled in America soon discovered that the Indian could never be metamorphosed into slavs and therefore did not attempt to make them such.

[p. 50]
It was owing to this haughty spirit of independance that those nations which did not remove to the westward but remained on alotments of land among the white people have dwindled away almost to nothing. The Indian like the Elephant will not propagate his race in slavery or even in any subordinate situation. Like the young duck he perishes alike by good or ill usage.

It was patriotism which led Tutela with his family and the remnant of his little nation to seek an asylum in the distant forests of the west with the lofty ranges of the Alegheny mountains between him and the conquerors. H wished to preserve his people from extermination and to live in his posterity.

What is this patriotism which leads to deeds of valor and even to those of desperation and so often effectually destroys our native dread of death? Is it the ambition of the Patriarchal honor of living in our offsping 'till time shall be no more? Is it the wealth honour science power glory freedom and antiquity of the nation concentrated in one ideal focus and poured upon the generous heart which considers the whole inheritance as its own? Is it then to be wondered at that the defence of this sacrad treasure is considered as the greatest duty of life? If the interests of our country can be advanced by life it is well but if those interests should require the sacrifice of life on the altar of patriotism it is as well the obligation of duty in either case is the same. Such is the sentiment of all those generous souls who are worthy of a home and a country.

[p. 51]
This love of country seems the strongest in those barbarous nations whose countries owing to their high

solitude of situation seem to be least worthy of such devotion. The Greenlanders Esquimaux and Kamschdales think their sterile regions the only places on earth where human happiness has placed her abode and tho' subsisting almost exclusively on the productions of the ocean and doomed to pass the dark half the year in filthy caverns they never can be persuaded to emigrate from their native land.

Oh! Patriotism! Thou adamatine bond of union amongst men. Thou dost associate in one aggregate focus the wisdom strength and ambition of those great and potent nations whose councils are felt and whose destructive operations carry bloodshed and devastation thro' every quarter of the globe. Thy associating influence is equally felt by the poor untutored savage whether he shivers in the bitter cold of Nova Zemble or half naked he parches beneath the burning sun of the desert of Zahara! Thy potent influence destroys the native fear of death in the breast of the warrior as he rushes into battle in the midst of the deadly machinery of war! 'Tis on they altar sacrad love of Country that the self immolated victim makes his offering as he conducts the forlorn hope Like that of the pass of Thermopylae steers the fire ship or calmly sits viewing his burning vessel till the explosion of his magazine blows him to atoms.

[p. 52]
While thy potent thunder is heard in worthy lightning flashes in the oratory of the statesman in senate of his nation Like the christian hope thou art strong in deth. The Stesman and the soldier as he breaths his last heaves a sigh for the wellfare of his country.

To the purest patriotism Tutela joined that noble endowment denominated disinterested goodness. He lived he toiled and suffered for the good of others without any prospect of reward other than that of a good conscience the esteem of his cotemporaries and the grateful remembrance of posterity.

Say Good Chistians is not this disinterested goodness the cardinal virtue of your religion? Was it not this the lovely virtue of the Good Samaritan whose benevolence made him a "Neighbour to all the world so that he lost sight of his own national character and personal interest in the sufferings of the wounded bleeding friendless fellow being whom he found on the high way? If there be any such things as works of supererogation they are not prayers acts of self mortification or pilgrimages. They must be deeds of benevolence in which forgetting himself the good man lives labours suffers or even dies for the benefit of others. Such was the Messiah and such were the first embassadors of his holy faith. The master had no where to lay his head the apostles

[p. 53]

Some time after the Powhattan confederacy of Indian nations was broken up by the first warlike adventurers into the Colony of Virginia a small remnant of one of those nations settled at a place on the Palava Sepa or Ohio river at a place afterwards denominated The Old Mingo Towns.

This place was quite remote from all the villages Indians in the same regions which were mostly situated far to the north and west of this little broken nation of Winnepecks for that was their name. The little assemblage of wigwams which sheltered these few Indian families was situated at first in a low valley on the west side of the river which is a stream of considerable magnitude but whose waters tho' gentle in their current instead of being clear like the rivers east of the Alegheny are are always of dark hue. This gloomy aspect of the river together with a considerable tract of low swampy land a little below the Town where a considerable stream discharges itself into the river as well as many other circumstances of the surrounding scenery were calculated to afflict the minds of these emigrants from a more delightful region with all the melancholy sensations of the exile.

The whole country on either side of the rver presented a dull monotonous aspect of broken hills of but small elevation. These hills were seperated from each other by dark gloomy ravines

[p. 54]
which for ages had been wearinng deeper by the torrents of rain which had gushed down the sides of hills. Even the river itself had sunk far below its former bed. This is known by the great height of its first alluvial banks.

At the foot of the hill on the east side of the river and nearlly opposite their Town these adventurers found a cavern among some large rocks containing many human bones. This place had been used by the first inhabitants of the country a sepulchre for their dead but this race of people like many nations of the old world had vanished from the earth*. This hallowed place they selected as a cemetery for their dead where their bones might repose with those of fellow beings of remote and unknown antiquity.

The surrounding woods in the unaltered state of nature were well stocked with the wild beasts of the western regions. The Buffaloe the Bear and the Deer furnished a plentiful supply of meat for this little settlement and in addition to flesh the river and ponds furnished them with a number of those fowls which nature has taught to dip the wing in water. The river gave a good supply of fish which altho of the coarser kind served to make an agreeable variety in

*In splitting stone for building a bridge over the mouth of Cross Creek an opening was found among some large rocks which contained twenty seven sculls with other corresponding bones. The author saw several of those sculls. From their shape it is evident that they were the sculls of Indians and from their exhibiting no marks of violence it presumable they were not the skeletons of persons slain in battle but of those belonging to some neighbouring town whose inhabitants this cavern as a common burying place.

[p. 55]
the food of those exiles from their native land. The bottom land on which they had fixed their residence was well adapted to the culture of the indian corn the seed of which together with that of squashes and beans they had brought with them. Their clothing consisted of the skins of beasts taken in the chace dressed and made up after the rude manner of ancient and barbarous times. Their wigwams were made of poles piled upon each other and covered with the bark of the ash trees. Their beds were shaggy bear skins placed on dry leaves with a covering of deer skins.

Thus in the primeval state of mankind these poor people lived for some years with but little intercourse with the rest of the world. They were poor but had enough and were contented little dreaming that the devastations of war inflicted by the merciless white men would ever reach their distant and lonely abode. Fatal security!

The chief of this tribe Tutala was pretty well advanced in years when with the remnant of his people he fled from oppression and sougt independence in this sequestered spot. A wife whose virtuous and correct deportment would have done honour to the most enlightened state of society a son and daughter constituted the whole of the family of the Chief of the Winnepicks.

As the most polished state of society produces a great many fools knaves and

[p. 56]
and vicious people who desire no improvement from ...gation but who owing to a natural defect of the constitution of the mind or the prevalence of some untoward passion or propensity to sensual indulgence are never brought under the dominion of reason but throughout life are the victims of ignorance and consuming vice in spite of the light of science and the good examples with which they are every where surrounded so in the barbarous State of society a few have exhibited to the world a genrous strength and cultivation of mind towering far above the humble circumstances of their birth and situation in life so that altho unaided by scholastic education by observation alone they as to every subject which falls within the range of their experience or traditional information concerning ...cuts of past ages they become philosophers statesmen or poets. Homer and Ossian were not scholars. The ages in which they lived were barbarous. Yet their songs much impaired no doubt by having been having been handed down thro' several generations before they were committed to writing are still ranked amongst the master pieces of poetic composition. The former was not inferior to Virgil Horace or Juvenal altho' they obtained their education in the zenith of the Augustean age. Perhaps America has not as yet produced a more accomplished orator than the famous but unfortunate Logan.

Of this latter description was Tutela. He was quite young when the European landed on the shores of his native country. This was an event which struck the population with utter astonishment. The report of a people with white skins coming in large canoes from over

[p. 57]
ingaged in the awful work of converting the world Without purse or scrip". Good men! Leights of the world! Benefactors of our dark and depraved nature 'till time shall be no more. Ye have your reward in Heaven.

    Let us not suppose that the Cardnal virtues of our nature do not exist among Pagans. The best examples presented by the Messiah for our imitation were taken not from the Jewish nation but from the Gentile world. It is the maternal affection and the firm faith of the poor Syrophenecean woman who applied him to cure her afflicted daughter. The good Samaritan pouring oil and wine into the bleeding wounds of the half murdered man who had fallen among thieves the good Centurian who prayed to God alway and gave much alms to the people whose blessed examples the New Testament so earnestly presses upon our attention.

    Tutela altho continually distressed with a strong presentiment of the utter extermination of the Indian nations by the whites thought it his duty to do every in his power to prevent or at least retard the event. He however concealed this apprehension from his little nation and even from his own family. Under his direction every thing was done indicative of an intention to make this retreat a permanent residence. The wigwams were built in the best manner a sufficient quanty of land was cleared and planted with corn and other vegetables. A small council house was built which as usual with the Indians aswered for a council hall and a temple of worship.

[p. 58]
In this hall the respectable image of the Maneto was put

up in its proper place before which the customary rites were duly perforformed and councils of the chief men of the Village with Tutela at their head were regularly held a war post was set up to signify that they were ready for self defence if occasion should require it.

Tutela and his people were in possession of a few muskets and fowling pieces which they had obtained from the English. These fire-arms they had learned to use with tolerable skill but as their stock of ammunition was but small they generally used the ancient weapons of their forefathers the bow and arrow in the chace for game. The few articles of English clothing which they had brought with them did not last long so that with but few exceptions they were all in the original dress of the ab-origines of America which consisted wholly of the skins of the beasts of the forest.

The elderly part of the Indians at the discovery of America by the whites thought it stupid in the Indians to dress in cloths made by the whites. It was an attrocious departure from the customs of their forefathers whose religious institutions like those of many other nations had prescribed the costume of their people. Immemorial custom at least had prescribed the mode of dress of the sexes that of the peace and war chiefs as well as that of common men. The young people however as is always the case in similar circumstances prevailed against the prejudices of the aged. They would be fine notwithstanding the murmurs of the aged.

Tutela altho' a man of superior understanding partook in a considerable degree of this anntipathy to

[p. 59]
the use of English fabricks in the dresses of the young Indians nor was he fond even of the guns as both the one

and the other served to remind him of the defeat and dispersion of his people. With regard to the use of them however he was by no means strenuous Particularly the latter which he forssaw would soon supercede the use of the bow and arrow.

Chap. 2nd

The children of Tutela Oma and Nuza were educated by their parents in the Indian manner with the greatest care and attention. Oma being the heir apparent of the little monarchy was early in instructed in all the leading maxims of the barberous policy of the indian nations with regard to warfare. Among the first exercises of the organs of speech of young prince were the war whoop the alarm yell the scalp and death halloo. Let not the white man smile at this branch of the Indian education. To them it is all important in war. The Indian is taught to utter yells which can be heard at a great distance and in such a manner as to have an appalling effect. At the onset of battle these terrific yells like martial musick of civilized nations seem to occasion an oblivion of death inspire courage and regulate the movements of the conflict. The different modulations of the voice in those yells answer answer all the purposes of the drum the trumpet the tocsin and alarm guns among the white nations.

Besides the war whoops an Indian must have the faculty of imitating the sounds of every bird and beast in the forest. An Indian who cannot deceive even the owls deer Wolves and

[p. 60]
wild turkies would not be thought an Indian of an accomplished education nor could he be a successful hunter.

The martial yells and languages of birds and

beasts were mastered by Oma at an early period. Being a well grown athletic boy he soon became adroit and skillful in the use of the bow and arrow. His Astronomy was that of directing his course by the sun in the day time and by the north star at night. In cloudy weather the height and thickness of the moss and bark on the north side of the trees taught him the cardinal points. He was taught to ascertain the course of the winds by holding his finger in his mouth until it became wet and warm and then holding it above his head. The side which first became cold was the windward side.

    Hunting and war were not the only sciences which Tutela taught his son Oma who being a prince required an education to qualify him for the monarchy of his little nation. The art of negotiation in peace and war was made known to him. The construction and interpretation of wampum belts must be understood by a chief among the Indians. These belts are made of the sinews of the deer and the quills of porcupines. The quills by their different colours and figures answer all the purposes of the art of writing among civilized nations.

    Amongst the Indians the chief has no revenue to support his houshold to pay or furnish his troops. In the chase in building the wigwam as well as in war he must personally take the lead. Hence he is rather a Patriarch than

[p. 61]
a monarch of his nation. Such were the lessons of instruction given by Tutela to his son Oma.

    Tutela in the education of his son carried his views beyond the ordinary qualifications of a chief in peace and war. He gave him the whole history of the arrival of the white people in America. He described their ships cannons houses implements of tillage and clothing. This history was in the highest degree interesting to the children of Tutela for it was as marvelous to Nuza as it was to Oma. The old man however always closed his narratives with the expression of the painful apprehension that these white people would in the end occasion the destruction of the Indian nations and that if the Indians wer intended to recover their country and independence there was no time to be lost.

  These narrations fired the ambition of Oma. He wished and prayed to the great Spirit that he might be made the deliverer of his country.

  At the age of Eighteen Oma made known to his father his wish to endeavour to unite the Indian nations for their deliverance from the presence and oppressions of the white men and candidly asked him whether he thought the scheme practicable.

  To this the old chief replied "My son I shall soon leave you the sole war chief of a small nation of poor Indians who have been much reduced in number and robbed of their country by the white skins. We are brave warriors but what is bravery without force. We are like the rattle snake who can indeed bite but he bites but once. He is instantly killed. I do not say that the Indian nations are not strong enough to drive away those strangers from

our country or kill them all. We could find warriors enough to beat them even with bows and arrows in spite of all their big guns which make thunder and lightning but can we be brought together? We are like a bundle of sticks strong when tied together but weak when pulled apart. These white people have the policy of pulling us from each other. They make peace with one nation and war with another so make the Indians kill one another. If they are let alone much longer they will be too strong for us all.

The magnitude of the scheme for expelling the invaders filled the immagination of Oma with the prospect of the most romantic atchievments. Young and inexperienced the little thought of the difficulties suggested by his father. He felt confident that the Indian nations only wanted a leader to unite them in one common cause to expel the invaders of their country.

A thirst for knowledge occupied the mind of Oma. He notwithstanding his youth felt regret that he knew so little of the world concerning which he had heard so much. He therefore resolved to spend some time in travelling first among the Indian nations to the west and north then among the nations east of the Alegheny and if circumstances should allow among the settlements of the white people on the shores of the great water.

Oma communicated his design of travelling to his sister Nuza. Fired with his project she resolved to be his companion in his travels and asked his permission to do so. To this request he gave his hearty assent.

The only remaining obstacle to the

[p. 63]
execution of the plan of Oma and his sister Nuza was that of obtaining the consent of their parents who being well advanced in years dauted much on their two children.

Their plan being stated to their father and his consent to its execution asked for Tutela requested time for deliberation. The young people were well assured of his compliance. An Indian seldom opposes any obstacle to the will of his children from an apprehension that by doing so he would spoil the independence of their minds and become responsible for their future worthlessness.

At the time appointed by Tutela he called his son and daughter and gave his assent to their request for permission to travel. In doing this he manifested all the studied apathy of the Indian charaacter. "We are old said Tutela and you are our only children you wish to leave us and make a long journey. It is likely we shall never see you again but the manito has put this into your hearts. It may be for the best. We have been young like you and then our parents allowed us to do what we thought best. We will now do so by you in hopes that it will be for the best. If you cannot deliver our people from the hands of the white men you will at least get some knowledge of the world.

Chap. III
The preparations for travelling

The Indian never sets out on a journey without preparations of a physical and religious

[p. 64]
nature. The charge of both these Tutela took on himself. Oma was provided with the best gun belonging to the nation and also with a liberal share of the little ammunition which they had among them to these were added the best suits of clothing which could be procured for him and his sister together with the best boes and arrows which the nation could furnish. A day not far distant was set apart for the religious ceremonies requisite for their consecration for their departure Ceremonies which the Pagans consider essential to safety and success in any important enterprize.

The day before the appointed feast of expiation

every person belonging to the little nation above the age of twelve years not only kept fast for one day but took a full dose of indian jabysick or poison root to purge off together with the contents of the stomach and bowels all the sins of their past lives.

The day of the feast was about the ful moon the begining of roasting-ear time. The hunters had killed some young bucks and other game for the solemn occasion. A fire was kindled early in the morning on the summit of a hill which overlooked the town on the west side for the purpose of burning the legs heads and hearts of the bucks together with some green corn as an offering to the great Manito. This service was performed by Tutela who was the high Priest as well as the monarch of his little nation.

[p. 65]
The offering made with the usual invocation by Tutela on behalf of his children his nation and himself the feast began and continued until evening and ended first with civic and then a war dance. The feast lasted seven days.

The civic dance was accompanied with a large drum made of a hollow log over one end of which a piece of deer skin with the hair grained off was stretched and secured with a hoop. This drum was beat by the old men in succession. The performer siting a straddle of the log produced his musick and regulated the movements of the dance by beating the head of the drum with two sticks. This drum was accompanied on the part of the performer with vocal musick and a song. If there was but little melody in this singing there was time measured by its emphasis and cadence the Indian wants no more. In addition to the musick of the drummer a number of the dancers were provided with gourds the shells of squsheres or bladders with pebbles in them. With these they rattled so as to keep time with the great drum. The dance was of that kind which is called <u>flat</u>-foot which consists of stamping on the ground seven or eight times first with one foot and then with the other. At every change of the foot the opposite arm is thrown round so ... the hand across the small of the back. The bodies of the dancers are

[p. 66]
considerably inclined forward and standing in straight lines present a regular curvature when viewed lengthways. Each dancer utters some humdrum modulations of the voice during the whole time of his exercise. This gives him further assistance in keeping time. This feast lasted seven days.

This feast with the dances which accompanied it was a religious observance a publick thanksgiving to the Manito for the new corn and other productions of earth for their support and imparted a solemn consecration those fruits. It was equivalent to the feast of Tabernacles among the Hebrews.

On the morning of the Eighth day after the commencement of the feast Tutela ascended the same hill on which the feast had been held for the purpose of performing his private devotions to the Great Spirit for the protection of his children now about to leave him and perhaps forever.

Having kindled a small fire he threw some kinnikrick into it and then commenced his prayer: "O thou great Manito I have made you an offering as I have done all my life for I have always worshiped and trusted in you and you have always answered me and protected me.

Now I beseech you hear Tutela again. He has grown old and feeble and cannot live much longer. As to himself, Tutela could die with contentment but he is distressed for his people who have been made few in number poor and driven from their country on the other side of the great mountain by the white people who have come across the great water

[p. 67]
where the sun rises in the morning. If it be thy will that the red people should all die and be forgotten we cannot help it. It may be that our day is gone and our night come but Tutela hopes not. He hopes that your red children will yet find means to kill these bad strangers, or drive them from our country.

O Good Spirit my children have undertaken to travel a long journey among the Indian nations and then among the white to see if our enemies or if not to find out a good country far away where the sun sleeps at night where our little nation may live and die in peace and hear no more of these white men. Give my children plenty of game on their jour and let them not be sect but right well and strong. Save them from the bites of snakes and from the panthers wolves and bears and Oh! Great Manito Tutela beseeches you with his eyes full of tears that he may live to see his children come home again.

Just as Tutela had finished his devotions the sun arose over the hill on the east side of the river while the river and the valleys above it were covered with a thick fog. The rays of the sun darted down into the fog in beautiful streamers less and less brilliant till they were lost in the darkness below. The upper surface of the cloud of fog which filled the space between the hills on each side of the river resembled the western clouds in a summer evening. It was finely tinged with white yellow and blue in the most fanciful

[p. 68]
figures.

Tutela although his heart was sad rejoiced to see sun and the grand appearance of his rays in rolling vapour below him and standing erect with his face towards he thus addressed the fountain of light

O! Sun who was made by the great and good Manito to give light to the world which without thee would be good for nothing. While thou sleepest far to the west a cloud of darkness comes over the ground and the eyes of every living thing are put out in the death of sleep. The moon and stars then sneak out of their darkness and shew their little light because thou are gone to rest but their light is too weak for our eyes. Thou wakest up in the morning and the stars go into their dark wigwams again. Thy first light falls on the eyes of the Indian as he lays asleep on his bear skin over his bed of dry leaves. He opens them gapes stretches himself and is alive again. The turkey as he sits on the limb of the high tree stretches out his long neck and flaps his wings gobbles and then flies to the ground. The bear buffaloe and dear rise from their beds of leaves stretch their limbs and begin to search for food. The little birds begin their song among the branches of the trees. The blossoms which had shut up their leave at thy going to sleep now open them again to catch thy first light. O! Sun thou art the light and the life of the world. A few ears of corn and a few snows have made Tutela old and feeble but thou art still young as thou wast when Tutela was young and when Tutela shall close his eyes in death

[p. 69]
and see thy light no more Thou wilt still be young. O! May Tutela and his children like thee be faithful in the station appointed them by the great Maneto.

Tutela having finished his prayers to the Maneto and his address to the Sun descended from hill just as his people with the feast and dances of the Seven last days had risen from their Slumber and lighted up the fires in their wigwams.

Contract

~~1819 October 5th 1819. This day contract with Captn. Benjn. Russell for his Crop of Cotton (about 11 Acres) to be delivered in town at a gin in good Merchantable order, at three Cents per pound, for which I am ... a Certain Nite Go Curling has ag^v him, the balance to remain about two Months after the last delivery.~~ J. W. Fleming Present.]

Dd. Chambers   Tomlinson Pontius
... Walkers   109 Dearborn St.
Doddridge

Notes & References on Doddridge's *Notes*

Latin quotations
    p. 65
    " 106

Hist. Seneca Co. 6
abt. Van Metre?

Cornstalk
    see Maj. Ths. Shelby's notes vol. 2d Trip 63

Cornstalk's widow
   Trip 63, p. 66 of Vol. 4

[p. 70]
P. 2d "To the reader"
   near bottom — abt. Noah Zane's Mss.

[p. 71]
Greek revolution, p. ix Preface
Preface x. Epaminondas &c. (spelled right?)
"   xi. Harmer?
   At the period when Dr. Doddridge wrote, 1823-'4, the public sympathies in this country, as the Editor well remembers, were strongly Excited with reference to the struggling Greeks in their war of Emancipation from Turkish thraldom, & vessels freighted with aid and comfort were sent them as the free-will offerings of the Amn. people. After many vicissitudes, Greek independence was acknowledged.

Teter — bear adventure — note	p. 21
Kinnekenick	26
{Grave Creek Mound, since opened	29
{ size, 28. See A.D. Tomlinson's statement.)	
~~Groupes, p. 29, 16th line from bottom~~	
Egyptian Superscriptions	31
~~Plaister? p. 31 in note, reliet? do.~~	
Sandwich Islands	33
Crim Fantasy	35
Inscriptions found in Md.	36
~~relicts? relies? line 12th~~	
{Indn. picture writing	37
{ see Schoolcraft	
Indn. copper implements	37

p. 49: Since Dr. Doddridge's day, a very large number of vocabularies of North & So. Am. Indn. languages have been reduced to writing, & many of them published, so that there is no danger of their vanishing from the knowledge of the world.
~~p. 49: "pawaws" or priests? 7th line from top.~~
p. 49: Angikoks. See last leaf for note.

[p. 72]
~~p. 50: rete mucosus 4th & 8th line from bottom & 4th & 5th from top, p. 51 ... 3d line from bottom?~~
~~p. 52: rete mucosum, see ... page 53: Do~~
Capt. Ths. Wells   62
p. 86: have summer heats increased since 1824? Doubtful.
p. 68: Fatal bite of mad wolf; cite Nall's case.
p. 70: Bees migrate with advancing settlers.
p. 77: Rattlesnake bite; Mrs. Singer's case.
p. 78: Rattlesnake bite; Ths. Edgington.
+ 84: <u>Service</u> trees; see separate slip note
+ 86: buckberries; see note on last page.
p. 94: Young Dunkard aids in rescuing Mrs. Glass?
    99: Settlements reached the Ohio in 1771; cff. note earlier.
    105: South Sea dream; Explain.
    110: Alex. Wells

[p. 73]
p. 110: delft ~~(3d line)~~? See separate note.
p. 112: give Dr. D's extract of visit to old tavern, in Memoir p. 32.
p. 113: Fisk.
    ~~114: Mocasson~~

~~claps knife (... clasp~~
~~114-15: Leggins~~
~~116: Shoe Pack~~
~~p. 120: Hobbles; 7th line from bottom~~
~~121:   "   4   "   "   top.~~
Saml. Teter hunting camp   132
~~p. 127: leggings; 12th line from top.~~
~~p. 133: "infuse"; 10th line from bottom.~~
p. 143: Egyptian dhoura bread: ~~on~~ 7th line fr. top
    184   do.   6   "   "
p. 148: wall-ink? (See Book on Useful Plants & Herbs.
  "   Epicacuanha = 4th from bot.
  "   pocoon; 3d/ fr bot.
p. 149: Plantain; see letter of Anderson, abt. E.R.C's
    statement of toad eating plaintain.
  See also Cuppis & Edgington's Notes.

  The early pioneers of the West did not appear to have been aware of the Efficacy of Spiritous liquor for the bite of poisonous reptiles. This is a more modern, & invaluable, discovery.

  151: snake bite; pig blind, Spring '43.
  160: Singing; Braddocks, Pt. Pleasant; Ms. Rooney;
    Crawford's; St. Clair

[p. 74]
p. 170: Nicknames to short cering soldiers;
    Dungfragrun; note Budy's
170-71: Whipping = McDonald's Sketches;
    ~~Nathn. Boone's Notes, abt. 98.~~
  Trip 1863, Vol. 1, p. 120 (Wm. Grant's Notes)
p. 174: ~~word faded out; bottom line~~: 181: conformation?
  "   convicts or indented servants; make note.
~~187: Alleghany 12th from bot.~~
190: Esprit de corps?; 9th from bot.

191: Mahommedan? 7th fr. top.
195: Note of Revs. Josh. Smith, John McMillen,
& Rev. Mr. Bowers.
197: orde of <u>St. Trap?</u>

French war:
218: Dalzell
" 100 men escorting provisions?
" Ecayer?
219-20: Wyoming needs a note
220: Paxton massacre &c.   221
221: Muddy Creek &c.
224: Refer in note to other parts of that war;
Boquests & Bradstreets Exp

[p. 75]
Dunmore's War
125: Peace - quasi bet. 64 & 74
233: Perogue
Wappatonika Campaign:
241: Col. Angus McDonald; give sketch
244: Ft. Laurens
246: Col. Clark; note.
248: Maj. Vernon
258: word blotted near bottom
256: 5th l. from bot.: Buckongehelas.
262: Moravians sent to Ft. Pitt late in '81; make
note of some killd. on Island.
265: Names of those who favored Saving the
Moravians: Col. Wmson, M. S. Wells,
Maj. McGuire
267: First prisoner taken in Spring burned; 7th
line fr. bot.; Note abt. M. Wetzel's
friend Wolf, see Jac. Wetzel &c.
309: Hoppus straps.

[p. 76]
Note p. 49.

The superstitious Greenlanders pay great respect to their angekoks, or sorcerers, who are at the same time their priests and physicians. L.C.D.

p. 86. Buck-berry: this is properly bog-berry, a species of oxycoccus, a name of the cranberry growing in low and marshy places. L.C.D.

[p. 77]
Invoices for cotton traded at Tuscaloosa Falls, Ala.

Rec No 18th 1819 of M. David Buck for Mr. W. Croft Eleven Balse Cotton as follows:

	No. 1. 242	No. 6 256
	2. 266	7 245
	3. 245	8 242
P	4. 260	9 224
	5. 264	10 249
	1277	11 220
	1436	1436
	2713 lb	

Gave Recp

Rec Nov 26th 1819 of M David Bucke five Bales Cotton as follows:

	No. 12 278	No. 15 296
	13 287	16 284
P	14 277	580 lb
	842	
	580	
	1422 lb	

No Recpt
Above # 1 to 16

1820
Jany 4th Sent all the Above 16 bale to Mess. Sheffield & Leaven by M. Penn Taylor

[p. 78]
Rec Nov 27th 1819 of Gustavus Hendrick Ten Bale Cotton as follows

	No. 1	265	No 7	228
	2	253	8	230
	3	240	9	239
	5	265	10	247
A				
	6	232	14	272
		1255		1216
				1255
				2471

Gave Recps #1 to 10

Rec Decr 9th 1819 of Gustavius by M Croft Nineteen Bales Cotton as follows

No 4	231	No 17	275	No 24	257
11	267	18	236	25	252
12	272	19	256	26	229
13	289	20	278	27	256
15	250	21	278	28	254
16	277	22	250	29	241
	1586	23	250		1489
			1823		1823
A	#10 to 29				1586
					4898 lb

Decr 21, 1819 Sent all the above by the Dispatch Capn. Hammonds To T. L. Hallitt

[p. 79]
Rec. Dec. 20th 1819 of John Thomas Sixteen Bales Cotton by Isaac Condry & John W. Williams as follollows

```
       269    323    271    274
  R    265    270    330    269
       286    289    255    308
       262    882    271    273
       261   1343   1127   1124
      1343   2225 lb        1127
                           2251 lb
                           2225
#1 to 16                   4476
   Weight at the Gin       4438
                             38 lb
```

Gave Rec for the weight at the Gin & paid freight for 4438 @ 75 cts to waggones tho Cotton having rain on it was the cause of the over weight.

Rec Tuscaloosa falls D. 21 1819 of I Shaw from E Nash Gin 1 Bale Cotton
S   #1

Sent all the above by the Despatch Decr 21 18 Capn Hammonds to T. L. Hallett

[p. 80]
Rec Tuscaloosa falls Dec 22nd 1819 of Mr Gustavus Hendrick on Contracts Nineteen Bales Cotton as follows

Adam Fain Cotton				G. Hendrick low	
#30	259	35	252	#39	276
31	263	36	268	40	296
32	260	37	265	41	269
33	260	38	<u>227</u>	42	281
34	<u>257</u>		1012	43	301
	1299		<u>1299</u>	44	264
			2311 lb	45	276
				46	240
				47	246
				48	<u>249</u>
					2698 lb
					<u>2311</u>
					5009 lb

1820
Jany 4th Sent the above Nineteen bales to T. L. Hallitt by M. Penn Taylor
A #35 to 48

Rec Tuscaloosa Falls Dec 22 1819 of Drake F. Randolph Five Bales Cotton
    as follows
R   #17 327   B. G.
        18 336
        19 300
        20 333
        21 <u>301</u>
            1597

1820
Jany. 4th: Sent the above 5 bale to Mes Leaven & Sheffield by M. Penn Taylor

[p. 81]
Rec in Store of Mr. Rowland Tancrue Seven Bale Cotton for and on his account
JThomas   Weighing 2840 lb
R
Advan on & Charged this day
Rec Tuscaloosa Falls Dec. 31th 1819 of M David Buck on contract Six Bales Cotton as follows

	D. Buck	No. 19	302	
		18	287	
		23	281	
		21	271	
		20	303	
	have Square	17	<u>290</u>	Rops &c
			1734 lb	

P #17 to 22
1820
Jany ...th Sent the above Six bales to Mess Leaven & Sheffield by M. Penn Taylor

[p. 82]
Rec Tuscaloosa Falls Dec 31 1819 by Drake F. Randolph five Bales Cotton as follows

R	#22	326	
	23	318	13th
	24	288	
	25	312	
	26	<u>290</u>	
		1534 lb	

Giv Note 10th July
$351.78

Rec Jany 3rd 1820 of Mr. David Buck by Thompson Team Eight Bales Cotton as follow

```
Nos. 28    //29    229
    30     30     286
    27     23     280
    26     24     242
    25     25     278
    24     26     297
    22     27     280
    29     28     273
                  2165 lb
```

1820
Jany 4th Sent all the above bales 13 in number to Leavem & Sheffield by M Penn Taylor

[p. 83]
Rev Tuscaloosa falls Jany 10th 1820 in Store of Mr. M. M. Harris by Mr. Easten & Croft fourteen Bales Cotton as follows

```
1 Bale  382}
1  "    335}   these bales were sold by Mr. Kirby
1  "    321}   to Mes B & G. Cox
1  "    346}
1  "    328}
        1712
1 Bale  360          Delivered W. S. Croft by Order
▷      #1 Bale  322}
21      1  "    324}
to      1  "    314}
28      1  "    335}   forwarded these bales
        1  "    317}   by Troy Hutton
        1  "    330}
        1  "    315}              1712
        1  "    325}               360
              2582 lb             2582
                                  4654
```

[p. 84]
Rev Tuscaloosa falls Jany 10th 1820 of Mr. J. Wood in Store by the hand of Mr. Adams & Rutherford Sixteen Bales Cotton as follows

Adams		Rutherford	
1 Bale	243	1 Bale	241
1 "	223	1 "	241
1 "	253	1 "	245
1 "	253	1 "	211
1 "	223	1 "	245
1 "	257	1 "	225
1 "	227	1 "	235
1 "	249	1 "	223
	1928 lb		1866 lb

Bot Tuscaloosa falls Jany 20th 1820 of Mr. James Childress Twenty Bales Cotton as follows, at 14 lbs.

△ #1	532	#8	392	#15	371
2	414	9	346	16	378
3	401	10	357	17	365
4	397	11	365	18	362
5	408	12	356	19	381
6	358	13	370	20	346
7	360	14	365		2203
	2870		2551		2551
					2870
					7624 lb

[p. 85]
Rev Tuscaloosa Falls Jany 21 1820 of Mr. David Buck on Contract by the hand of Mr. Wm. Croft & Mr. Phillips, Twelve Bales Cotton as follows

```
        Mr. Phillips      Mr. Croft
     #31      224      #41      237
   P  32      233       45      272
      33      233       46      264
      34      215               773
      35      264              2246
      36      293              3019 lb
      37      264
      38      258
      39      262
              2246 lb
```

Rev Tuscaloosa falls Jany 21st 1820 of Mr. Wm. Croft on Contract with him four Bales Cotton as follows

```
   P  #40   256}   this lot being mixed with Mr. Bucks;
       42   256}   the number have got disordered and
       43   292}   will continue as tho all had been Mr.
       44   254}   Bucks
            1058 lb
```

[p. 86]
Rev Tuscaloosa falls Jany 25th 1820 of Mr. John Thomas for Mr. Condey Seven Bales Cotton as follows

```
   R        #17      364
             18      303
             19      315
             20      361
             21      304
             22      354
             23      353
   Gav Ref           2354 lb
```

Rev Tuscaloosa falls Jany 25th 1820 of Mr. G. Hendrick by Ned on his Contract Ten Bales Cotton as follows

A	#49	248	#54	291
	50	278	55	250
	51	269	56	242
	52	258	57	248
	53	<u>229</u>	58	<u>256</u>
Gav Recp		1282		1287
				<u>1282</u>

Gave note 2nd March   2569 lb
& G B Leaven ...

			Hendricks	
#30	259		#39	276
31	263		40	296
32	260		41	269
33	260		42	281
34	257		43	301
35	252		44	264
36	268		45	276
37	265		46	240
38	<u>227</u>		47	246
	2311		48	<u>249</u>
		Dam Fair		2698

[p. 87]
Rev Tuscaloosa falls Jany 26th 1820 in Store of W. Truss by Mr. Stewart Seven bales Cotton as follows

W. Gorman				March 20th 1820
W. Truss	#1	281		The lot delivered Mr.
	2	294		Truss & Sold Mess.
	3	283		G & G. Saltonstall
	4	261		
	5	280		
	6	281		

Recpt 7 <u>301</u>
1981 lb

Rec Tuscaloosa falls Fabey 2 1820 in Store of Mes. Slauter & Galarpec by Steelman & W. ADory fifteen Bale Cotton as follow

E.B.	#1	312	9	262
S&G	2	269	10	268
	3	268	11	268 Steelman
	4	274	12	274
	5	311	13	264
Mr.	6	316	14	299} round
Adory	7	321	15	<u>282</u>}
	8	<u>305</u>		1917 lb
		2376 lb		

[p. 88]
Rev Tuscaloosa falls Feby 3d 1820 in Store of Col John Wood by Mr. Tarrence & Rutherford fourteen bales Cotton as follow, oraginal Weights

‡ Wood	268	273	292	283
	276	267	277	275
	291	250	300	
	291	289	275	

Gave Recpt

Recr Tuscaloosa falls Feby 3rd 1820 of Mes. A & Jenkin Gin Nine bales Cotton as follows

A & Jenkins	#34	252	44	260
	35	256	45	254
<u>P. Rempson</u>	36	266	46	278
	40	260		
	41	322		
By Shelton	42	282		

Rev Tuscaloosa falls Feby 5th 1820 ... Mr. Sparks & Co. for in good three Bales Cotton as follows

P   #   232
                224
                <u>235</u>
                691   ad 1210

[p. 90]

Notes & References on Doddridge's *Notes*

1846 — complete — Vol. 12
1851 — Complete — Vol. 17
   52   do
   53   Except Septr.
   54   Except Septr.
   55   complete
   56   do.
   57   Except Jan.
   58   "   Septr.
   59   "   Feb.
   60   "   Mar.

We have in Dr. Doddridges "<u>Notes</u>"
    Of the primeval forester, and his Singular habits, dress, occupations and amusements, we have ample accts. from the pens of various historians of the border; among these the first rank is due to Dr. Doddridge who relates that he saw and lived in the midst of.
         Southn. Lit. Messenger
Gulan's Leap, <u>May, 1856</u> — <u>Southn. Lit. Mess.</u>

Col. Dl. Boone, 1785- Jan. 1860.

Biographical sketch of Philip Doddridge, of Brooke County, Virginia. By W. S. Laidley
 [In The West Virginia Historical Magazine, January, 1902, p. 54-68]
 Contains genealogical data.

[p. 90[1]]
Receipt

THE AMERICAN EXPRESS CO. DO A GENERAL Express Business between all the Principal Cities and Towns of NEW YORK, KENTUCKY, WISCONSIN, WEST'N PENNSYL'IA, MICHIGAN, OHIO, ILLINOIS, MINNESOTA, INDIANA, IOWA, CANADA, And connecting with other responsible Expresses to All parts of the world.
American Express Company
Tem. Raul July 24 1868
Received of L. C. Draper _____ said to contain _____ valued at _____
_____ Dollars, Marked L. C. Draper Madison Wis
Which we undertake to forward to the nearest point of destination reached by this company, subject expressly to the following conditions, namely: This Company is not to be held liable for any loss or damage except as forwarders only, nor for any loss or damage by fire, by the dangers of navigation, by the act of God or of the enemies of the Government, the restraints of Government, mobs, riots, insurrections, pirates or from or by reason of any of the hazards or dangers incident to a state of war. Nor shall this Company be liable for any default or negligence of any person, corporation or association to whom the above described property shall or may be delivered by this Company, for the performance of any act or duty in respect thereto, at any place or point off the established routes or lines run by this Company, and any such person, corporation or association is not to be regarded, deemed or taken to be the agent of this Company for any such purpose, but on the contrary, such person, corporation or association shall be deemed and taken to be the agent of the person, corporation or association from whom this Company received the property above

described.

Nor shall this Company be liable for any loss or damage of any box, package, or thing, for over $50, unless the just and true value thereof is herein stated; nor upon any property, or thing, unless properly packed and secured for transportation, nor upon any fragile fabrics, unless so marked upon the packages containing the same; nor upon any fabrics, consisting of, or contained in glass. The party accepting this receipt hereby agrees to the conditions herein contained.

For the proprietors, _____, *Agent.*

Md 275

Letters from N. Doddridge to L. C. Draper

Wellsburg, Nov. 27, 1866

L. C. Draper, Esq.
Madison, Wis.

Your favor of the 26 inst. is to hand, and while much gratified to hear from you once more, I am quite at a loss to decide what response to make to your proposition to bring out a Second Edition of "Doddridge's Notes." I certainly feel very desirous to see the work in a new dress, and had not fully relinquished the hope of accomplishing the enterprise at some future day. Nothing but the want of adequate means to effect the object has hitherto prevented its execution. By some fatality, the Doddridge family have always been comparatively poor, not because they had not the ability to make money, but for want of the tact to keep it. After witnessing the triumphant departure to the Spirit-land of some of those most dear to me, in Ohio, and the marriage and dispersion of other members of my family, in 1862 I returned to the "Old Homestead" in this place, where, without desiring to do so, I have remained. In that year I commenced canvassing for subscribers to the "Notes", hoping to obtain a sufficient number to cover the expense of bringing out a new Edition; had gotten about six hundred, when the sudden rise in the cost of paper & other materials I found would quite if not more than cover the price at which I had offered the book, and of course I had to give up the enterprise at that time. My experience in the short canvass however, satisfied me that I could readily sell the work, more particularly where the family was known. During the past year, I have acted as agent for the sale of several recently published works and have not unfrequently been told that if I had a copy of my father's "Notes" it would be gladly purchased.

It was my intention to add to the "Notes," the history of the principal events which occurred at Wheeling and in the vicinity during the Indian War. Tell me if in your herculean researches after truth, you have found anything more reliable respecting the two sieges at Wheeling, than Withers & M'Kiernan give. In your "Circular," you mention that you had seen "Survivors of the Siege at that place in 1779." Did you receive and new light from them?

I have a "Memoir" partially prepared. It embraces unpublished historical facts in the rise and growth of the Ep. Church in Western Virginia & the Sate of Ohio in which he was a prominent actor, the facts being principally derived from his letters and correspondence. The Memoir, I wish to submit for revision &c. to some intelligent Episcopalian, but must seek one abroad, perhaps at Wheeling, there being none such here. Have a likeness also, drawn from memory, by an intimate acquaintance of the original.

To sum up, I cannot give you a definite answer at this time. I must have the "Memoir" perfected and the likeness put in a different shape, it being only in pencil, neither of which can be done here. Will consult my only surviving brother J. G. Doddridge, Sen. of Circleville, O. and write you again. I think that in within the next two weeks I can go to Wheeling and see if I can get the Memoir perfected. It will be breif, but may occupy two hundred pages.

Should like to know the cost of bringing out the work pr. Vol. in your place. I am now negotiating for the sale of some property here, wh. if I succeed in doing, I may be able to invest a few hundred dollars in the enterprise. Let me hear from you again.

    Resptflly & truly yours,
    N. Doddridge

[p. 92]

    Wellsburg, April 11th, 1866

L. C. Draper, Esq.
Madison, Wis.

Your letters of the 2 inst. are to hand, one of them arriving by today's mail. I wrote my brother the same day I wrote you 28 ult. making him acquainted with your wish regarding the "Notes", and also requesting a copy of the likeness but have not as yet heard from him possibly he may have been from home. To-day have sent him your subsequent letters as I desire his opinion and advice before giving a decisive answer. If you should edit the work, do you design adding thereto a history of the events at Wheeling &c? As a history of the Indian wars in Western Virginia it certainly is incomplete without this addition. Can furnish whatever you may desire. Will have to send the Manuscript copy of the Russian Spy not having a printed copy.

I may be mistaken in the number of pages the Memoir will occupy. It was merely guesswork when I said 200 pages.

Should like to have some idea of the first cost of the volume and the selling price feeling almost satisfied that I could sell more copies of it in this part of the country than any one else.

Will write you when I hear from my brother.

                With much respect
                Truly yours
                N. Doddridge

[p. 93]

                Wellsburg, May 19th 1866

L. C. Draper Esq.
D Sir

Yours of the 9 inst. reached me on the 12 but having to devote the preceding part of the week to superintending the seeding of a number of lots of ground, I could not earlier respond to it.

Mrs. Kirk has been dead some years. The name of her sister's husband was Wallace. All of them have removed to the West; could not learn their address.

Have written to a relative in Ross Ct Ohio who knew Captain Teter ... who I think died in that Ct. for the information you desire.

As I do not exactly know what items to send you for the Memoir I send instead the first draft of same I prepared several years ago from which you will be able to cull such facts as you may need. I send two Elegies which if you think proper may be appended to the Notes.

The Doddridge Captures, &c. you are at liberty to amend and abridge at pleasure.

Have not found a continuation of the Siege of 1777, at Wheeling & presume no more of it was written than the few sentences I sent you.

I have an account of M'Colloch Leap, derived from

the late Judg Scott of Chillicothe and Wm. Bukey who is still living, near Columbus, O., both of whom recieved it from the ... himself. An Acct. of a "Scouting party," also from Judge Scott and several other items in which Major John M'Collach was a prominent actor. If you wish these I will copy & send them.

I send 3 pages of the Russian Spy, all I find in my father's manuscript books, merely for your perusal.

The R. Spy was published in the Chillicothe Gazette, in 1825 & 6, when the Author was in Ohio, and I think it probable the manuscripts were not preserved. The letters were also published in a Hillsboro paper about the same period, edited by a Mr. Carothers, who was married to a niece of my father. Also, the "Narrative of John Bengemen."

Respectflly & truly yours,
N. Doddridge

P.S. It is ... for unnecessary for me to say that when you have done with the Memoir and the manuscripts of my father I wish them returned. The former I wish to rewrite as soon as convenient. Should be pleased to have your criticism upon it, suggestions, &c.

Have found nothing respecting Hardie, the hermit, in addition to What the Notes contain.

[p. 94]

Wellsburg, May 2, 1866.

L. C. Draper, Esq.

Indisposition must be my apology for delay in replying to yours of the 17 ult.

You have my consent to your proposition to edit a second Edition of the "Notes." I frankly confess that I have not arrived at this conclusion without reluctance. I wish the work republished, and doubt not you will do my father justice and add much to the original which will be interesting and valuable in a historical point of view. To no other individual than yourself would I have accorded this privilege had it been asked. I will send with this a copy of Logan. Will hunt up the Russian Spy, which, however, I think you will not use. It, with notes for a brief Memoir & the likess, which I wish to have improved by an artist, must be sent hereafter. Shall have to go to Wheeling to get this done as we have no artist here. Went to Steubenville for this purpose two days ago, but found the artist there unale to do any thing from a disease in his eyes.

Your publisher will probably do nothing until the tax on paper & printing materials is repealed, which there is good reason to believe the present Congress will do. When this is done the cost of publishing books must certainly be diminished.

Now I enjoin it upon you to arrange that I shall have the privilege of selling the book in West Va. Western P... & Ohio. It would be pleasant to me to supply those who subscribed for the Notes, besides this, the author of these was popular & in those parts well known, and I think one of his family wd. probably be more successful in selling the work than a stranger, especially if it was known that the family had some interest in it.

Let me hear from you and say whether you need the other documents immediately. I am still considerably indisposed, but will do the best I can to facilitate their readiness.

Your friend I. Brady Esq. is still in existence. Saw him last fall. He was hale and hearty and talked much of matrimony; jesting I presume. Have not heard of Mrs. Cruger's death, which I should probably have done had it taken place.

    P.S. I have a manuscrip copy of the murder and capture of members of the Doddridge family by Indians on the Monongahela in 1778 I think wh. I will send you for insertion in the Notes. It is brief, & was given principally by P. Doddridge, Esq.

                      Respfly & Truly yours,
                      N. Doddridge

[p. 95]

                Wellsburg, June 9th 1866.

L. C. Draper
Pheasant Branch
Dane Ct. Wis.

    Your last two letters are before me and make a series of interrogatories before I may succeed in making my ... intelligible to you.

    1. The "Stuart Narrative" you can retain until you are done with it. Would prefer having my father's papers entire.

    2. The "Memoir" I asked you to return. The Doddridge Narrative & Elegies I copied & you can retain them. Should like them to appear in the book. The narative you are at liberty to abridge.

    3. "Scouting party" and McColloch's Leap". Will send Manuscript Book containing them not now having time to copy. Anything relating to the McColloch family properly belongs to the early history of Western Virginia.

    4. "Captain S. Teter" I enclose a note from his grand son.

    5. Kirk family. Will, so soon as opportunity occurs, enquire of Mr. S. Jacob with whom Mrs. K. lived many years & at whose house she died. If I learn anything from him will communicate it to you.

6. "Father Quinn's Autobiography" can be had I presume at any Methodist Book Store. The Extracts I have were copied and sent me by a friend. Rev. J. B. Finley's autobiography might also be useful to you. He was one of the pioneers of the Methodist Ch. in the Western regions, but not so early in the field as Father Quinn. Both those were probably personally acquainted with Capt. Teter, but whether Finley mentions him or not I do not know. he labored much in Ross Ct. O. where Teter lived.

7. The Doddridge family were originally from Maryland. Philip, the brother of John, my grandfather, settled on the West Branch of the Monongahela in 1770. John took up land in Friend's Cove, a valley a few miles south of Bedford, Pa. where he remained till after the birth of his son Philip, May 17 1773, and soon after emigrated to Washington Ct. Pa. He must have left his native State prior to 1770 as my father was born in 1769, and as he himself states at Friends Cove, Pa. Thank you for calling my attention to the annachronism. I got the date of Philip's settlement on the Monongahela from his two nieces, mentioned in the Doddridge Narrative, but do not really know at what precise time my grandfather left Md. but his Bible, which I have, states that he was married Dec. 22nd, 1767, and his wife was a daughter of Richard Wells of that State. My father says in his Notes that he was sent to Maryland soon after his mother's death, which event occurred Nov. 20th, 1776, when he was but little over seven years of age. When I said he was seven, I supposed it would be understood that he was in his eigth year. 8. How long was gr father engaged in writing his Notes &c &c." I think he was not more than one year in writing and publishing them. I was absent from home 1 year & knew nothing of his design until he sent me a subscription paper or prospectus of the work. As to collecting

materials, he had probably been doing that all his life from those who were familiar with the events of the Indian War and many of them personally engaged in it. To understand this, I must tell you that my father had an extraordinary memory. He never forgot any thing that he saw or heard. I never saw any manuscript except the one I sent you, that of Col. Stewart. My father's health was fast declining when he prepared the Notes, and I am persuaded he felt it to be a duty incumbent on him to give to the public the facts which he had treasured up in his memory respecting the Indian war, and I have not a doubt of their correctness so far as they are presented by him. Had he entertained a hope of living even five years longer, when he commenced committing to paper his Notes, he would have doubtless solicited aid from others, but this he did not, and consequently prepared and put to press such facts as he possessed. I send for your perusal several letters which he wrote in 1824, the year the Notes were published, from which you will percieve that he had a presentiment that death was not far distant.

I know you differ from him respecting the "Cresap affair". In this matter he gave the view current in this region from the time the affair took place, and do not think that he knew they had been controverted. Had he been aware of this fact I think his attachment to the Cresap family and his relations to the Rev. J. G. Jacob, who married the widow of Capt. Cresap, would have led him, could he have done so without violating what he concieved to be the truth of history, to present the matter in at least a modified form.

9. "Errors in the Notes." In speaking of errors, I had ... to those only which would have been corrected on the proof sheets — typographical.

10. "The Manuscript Book" I shall send on Monday

or Tuesday next. Wish to send it to Steubenville for ... to save cost. With it I send the Mss. of an unfinished Indian novel, & some of my father's letters, all of wh. will give you some knowledge of the authors character of mind. Also a few pages wh. seem to be the commencement of his autobiography.

11. "Mr. Bukey." Mr. Bukey, now living 8 miles from Columbus, removed from Va. some years ago. He is the son of John Bukey, who was a brother of my mother, and thus is grand-son to Maj. M'Mahon, who fell at Fort Recovery. He is a very excellent man tho' partially uneducated. His father, John, & Hezekiah a brother of John were Spies under Capt. Brady of Indian notoriety. I do not know his P. O. address, but a letter wd. reach him thro' the Columbus Office, if you wd. so request. He cd. tell you much about Maj. John M'Colloch.

12. "P. Doddridge," Esq. Will send you in a few day a picture of him, at least such facts as will enable you to prepare a suitable notice of him. I knew him well, loved, nay, almost worshipped him, and ... desire such a notice of him in the "Notes" worthy of the excellency of his character. Hopy you will bear in mind that the "Memoir" itself is merely a statement of facts intended to be revised and rewritten. The Notes were merely reminders, also to be, som of them, and the one respecting P. D. in particular, to be extended. Should time and means allow I hope to have this Memoir, with some of my father's correspondence relating to Church matters, published. Could you not send me your sketch of the Author of the Notes when it is finished? Will promptly return it.

Could you not in some way intimate that the author's family have some interest in the publication of the Notes, or rather can you not make some arrangement with the publisher that we may have? You will deem the expression of such a wish presumptuous in me, but of course, I feel anxious that the enterprise should be a success, and my experience in canvassing for subs. satisfies me that an understanding of this kind would facilitate the sale of the work in the west.

I wish to send this by to day's mail & will ... send the Manuscript book to Steubenville to be expressed. Shall address it, as per request, to Middleton Station, &c.

In haste, Truly &c. &c.
N. Doddridge

[p. 96]

Dr. Doddridge, says Albach in his Annals of the West," has well described the manners & customs of its Early inhabitants".

Dr. Doddridge says Peck in his Life of Boone has given an exact and graphic portraiture of the backwoods hunter.

[p. 97]

Wellsburg, Nov. ... 1866.

L. C. Draper, Esq.
Pheasant Branch
Wisconsin

...

D Sir

... your letter of July 24 last but seem to ... to answer. I have delayed an answer much longer than I intended to as when it was recieved. Those had ... interested said ... sorry to ... in your behalf.

From a farmer, I obtained the address of one of the brothers Wallace, which you wished to have was told the other was dead. It is

Robert Wallace & Son,
Benton ... Town

... sketch ... to the disease of wh. he died, say of ..., which I doubt ...

I would suggest that ... against the Indians ...

There is an aged man Patrick Gass ... something of the ... Walker. He has been also but for some months but I am ... and home lately. Will try to see him & gain such information as I can.

... of whom I include some enquiries ... Capt. S. Teters said that if ... information concerning him, and he doubted not but he was ... supposing ... it yourself.

... to jot just a line, ... to have some 6 ... memory I applied to an artist in Steubenville, and to one who has recently come to ... The former had lost his eyesight, & the latter said he could not do it. Shall try in Wheeling when I go there.

When you have time to write, shall be happy to hear of your health and progress.

    Truly yours,
    N. Doddridge

[p. 98]

    Wellsburg, Nov. 12, 1866

L. C. Draper
Phesant Branch, Wis.
Dr. Sir,

More than three months have elapsed since I have had the pleasure of hearing from you, and cannot but fear that you have not recuperated in health. Wrote you on the 1 Oct., enclosing the address of Robert Wallace & Coln. John M'Donald, but have as yet recieved no answer.

Should very much like to know how you are progressing with the "Notes &c. Would say in this connexion, that if your Publisher hesitates about doing his part, it is possible I could procure one to undertake it without any loss to you.

Please favor me with a few lines now.

Truly yours,
N. Doddridge

[p. 99]

Wellsburg, Dec. 13 1866.

L. C. Draper

Since your last letter, July 24, in which you mentioned that you had had a series of ill spells, I have written you twice, but so far have recieved no answer.

Should indeed be glad to hear from you and to learn how you are progressing with the "Notes" ... In my last, I stated that if your publisher hesitates about bringing out the book, that possibly I could find one who would do it without any disadvantage to you. But of course, I have not felt at liberty to make any particular enquiries ignorant as I am of the arrangements you may have made. Do favor me with an answer on the receipt of this.

Truly yours,
N. Doddridge

P. S. If you have done with the manuscripts I sent you I should be glad to have them returned as soon as convenient. I wish to use some of them.

The book containing the draught of the Notes you can retain as long as it will be of any use to you.

I have not yet been to Wheeling, but now have leisure to go if you still wish to hear what Mrs. Cruger has to say.

[p. 100]
Wellsburg, Jan. 23d, 1867.
L. C. Draper
Pheasant Branch
Dane Ct. Wis.
Dr. Sir,
Yours of the 7 to hand. Very glad to hear from you once more but regret to learn that your health is not improved. I very much fear that if the publication of the "Notes" is postponed neither you nor I will have the pleasure of seeing the new Edition of them. The individual to whom I referred as probably being willing to cooperate in bringing out the work is not a publisher but has an interest in a large publishing house, in the West, and is extensively acquainted with the Book business. I am not certain that he would embark in the enterprise for I did not enter into any details did not even give him the name of the book, but, with your <u>permission</u>, would be more communicative. What will be the size of the volume, and the probable number of pages? I have little faith in the success of the Notes if they are brought out in the East, where they are known but to a few of the literati. But in the West the work is well known, as also its Author. Am I at liberty to say any thing more on the subject? Please let me hear from you soon.
In haste, Truly , &c.
N. Doddridge
It is the Memoir that I was most anxious to have, having leisure this winter to rewrite it. Any suggestions from you by way of improvement of the document will be gratefully recieved.
N.

[p. 101]

Wellsburg, Jan. 30, 1868.

L. C. Draper, Esqr.
Pheasant Branch
Wisconsin

I have long deferred acknowledgeing the receipt of the Memoir and your Note of May 26, '67.

My father died on the 9 Nov. 1826 as stated in the Memoir. My mother died on the 25 Sept. 1829. I never saw a record of their marriage, but from the age of their eldest son, they must have married in 1794 or 95.

Mrs. Cynthia Wells, whose address I sent you lived in Jefferson City, Missouri. I subsequently sent you, I think in Oct. 1866, the address of Col. John M'Donald, who lived in Ross Ct. Ohio, gave you the name of his Post Office, which I cannot now recal, as a person who would be likely to give you the desired information respecting Col. S. Teter. Mrs. Cruger is dead. I did not see her as you desired me to do. Had not my means been too limited I should have made special visit to her on your account.

My object in writing now is to request the favor of you at your earliest convenience to send me The small manuscript book — blue cover — and my father's letters 4 of which are addressed to his son P. B. Doddridge and 4 to my mother, Mrs. J. Doddridge. There was also, I think one page of comments of Rev. H. Lee, on the Memoir, but of this I am not certain. If it is among the papers, should like to have it. I find it named in list of papers sent to you in June 1866. The large manuscript book of my father's Notes I should like also to have, but if you have further use for it will not insist upon its being sent now. My father has a grand-son, now at Harvard College, who has talents and seems determined to make a mark in the world, for whom I desire to preserve all these papers.

We now have two Express Offices in this place, to one of which you can send the package.

I shall happy soon to hear from you and especially happy to learn that your health has improved.
Truly yours,
N. Doddridge.

[p. 102]
Wellsburg, Ap. 6th, 1868.
L. C. Draper
Madison, Wis.
Dr Sir,
Your favor of Mar.2 did not reach me till the 18th. I was preparing to answer it when that of the 26th came to hand Sat. last. I'm truly sorry, to learn that your health is not improved.

Have endeavored, but without success, to learn the date of Mrs. Cruger's death. It however took place late in Oct. or early in Nov. '67. Ascertained last year that I could not have the desired change made in the likeness in this place nor in Steubenville, and having some doubts whether it would be needed, did not go to Wheeling, where I presume it could be done, at considerable expense however to me, and being very scarce of funds, did not pursue the matter. But when certified that you will certainly need it, will make an effort to go to W. and have it prepared. When this is done, will also send an autograph. Have not been abl to find W. Lee's comments upon the Memoir & hope they may be found among the remaining papers. Not having heard of the death of your friend I. Brady, Esq. I conclude he is still among the living. Thus far in answer to the queiries contain in yours of

Mar. 2nd.

Have not found any manuscripts relating to the "Notes" except those I sent you. If there were others they were probably sent to the presiding officer & there left. I would not willingly cause you any extra haste or trouble, but I do really need the small book and the letters.

Mr. Gass is yet living and in this place. I visit him weekly, sometimes to read to him. He is now in his 97 year and entirely blind, but otherwise retains his faculties, and enjoys good health. He is cheerful, patient, fond of social converse, and seems to regret nothing so much as the loss of his sight, as he is thereby deprived of the pleasure of reading. He is in indigent circumstances, but is in the house of an affectionate daughter & kind son in law. The latter is afflicted with Epilepsy which frequently interrupts his daily labors for the benefit of his family.

I think I once mentioned to you that if the Notes were published in the East I should like to have the privilege of purchasing, at cost, as many copies as I could sell in the West, which would I think amount to some hundreds. Did you mention this to your publisher. I should like to know if such an arrangement can be made with him. During the past year I have had offers from three individuals to republish the "Notes" but could give no definite answer until I knew what your publisher would do.

Wishing you success in the pursuit of health & all other good things I am

     Truly yours
     N. Doddridge

P.S. Please let me hear from you as soon as convenient.
    N. D.

[p. 103]

Wellsburg, May 12, 1868.

Lyman C. Draper:
D. Sir,
    Your favor of 23 ult. also the book and letters are to hand.
    I regret to hear that your caput is in rebellion, but certainly think that such an extensive excursion as you have indicated in your letter will, at this delightful season, prove not only recuperative but replete with varied enjoyment. May your largest anticipations of sanative benefits therefrom, be more than realized.
    I had thought of amending several of the sketches contained in the manuscript book and offering them for publication. Should I do so, will notify you.
    Am sorry you did not give me the name of your publisher in Cinn. Was under the impression that he lived in the east.
    Should any thing occur to prevent the completion of your present intention with regard to the "Notes" I beg you will turn over to me the items you may have prepared for the work and I will if health and life be spared, accomplish it. Have some real estate which I would sell for that purpose. It now brings me little more than the taxes on it but in the hands of a better manager it would be profitable.
    Wishing you a pleasant and prosperous journey I am,
Very truly yours
N. Doddridge.

[p. 104]

Wellsburg, May 22 1869

L. C. Draper
Pheasant Branch
Dane Ct. Wis.

During the past Winter ... extremely desirous to have the manuscripts mentioned in my last letter, Jan. 23, and requested you to send me, not wishing to be troublesome, I forebore to renew the request, still flattering myself they would come.

I have now reason to regret my forbearance, as much of the information contained in the Memoir & letters is now called for by a Committee apointed by the last Con. of the Prot. Ep. Ch. of the Diocese of Ohio. The 50th or Jubilee Con. of that diocese meets June 5, to which it is to be presented. The request comes in the form of an invitation to attend the Con. & if I cannot do so to write &c. If the Memoir were revised and rewritten as I designed doing last winter I should send it, but even if you should send it at once there will not be time for this, but I may be able to make some extracts which will have to answer for the present.

Now I hope you will not after recieving this, delay an hour to send the "documents", all which I sent you except the large book which you can retain till you have done with it. Pay the Express chg. or I may not get the package for some days after it arrives at the Office.

In haste, yours &c.
N. Doddridge

[p. 105]

Wellsburg, June 28, 1869

L. C. Draper, Esq.
Madison, Wis.

Yours of the 12 inst. lay in the Office here some days before it was reseived. During the Spring I suffered much from successive colds, most of the time confined to my room, and neither desired nor sought for extraneous news. On Friday last the P. Master sent my mail matter to the house, and your letter made a part of it. When, 3 years ago, permission was given you to Edit and bring out a new Edition of the "Notes," it was confidently expected by the family that the work would appear in a reasonable length of time. In response to an enquiry from me in the summer of '66 as to the time of its appearance, you replied, you thought in the course of the ensuing Autumn.. During the second year after this permission was accorded you, several offers were made to republish the Notes which would have resulted in pecuniary advantage to the family, but in deference to you they were declined, altho' at the time, in consequence of your long delay and the infirm state of your health, we entertained but a faint hope that you would consummate the book. Since Ap. '68, till subsequent to the announcement of Clayton & Co., we never heard a word from you on the subject, and verily believed you had altogether relinquished the enterprise, and felt perfectly at liberty to make other arrangements, of which you would have been informed in due time. We feel quite satisfied that more than ample time has been allowed you for the completion of the work you undertook in the spring of 1866.

Owing to the altered curcumstances of several ... members of the Author's family, we now feel it is an imperative duty to endeavor to realize some pecuniary benefit from a reissue of their father's "Notes."

It does appear to me that there was no necessity for taking so much pains to hunt up information respecting the attack on Rice's Fort either corroborative or refutative of the account given of it by my father. He was 12 years of age at the time it took place, lived but a few miles from the Fort and was, in after years, well acquainted with the ... individuals who participated in its defence. It would have been far from agreeable to his family ... have seen his historical statements, so far as they go, made to appear dubious, by the insertion, in form of notes or otherwise, of counter relations. I ... regret that he was prevented by Mr. Zane from collecting the items of history connected with the various sieges at Wheeling, as they are very important ... the completion of the history of the Indian War in that part of Virginia.

Very Respectfully yours,
N. Doddridge

[p. 106]
Letter from George W. Remsen to L. C. Draper

Claxton, Remsen & Haffelfinger,
Publishers, Booksellers and Stationers
819 & 821 Market Street.

Edmund Claxton
George Remsen   *Philadelphia, May 20, 1869*
C. C. Haffelfinger

My Dear Mr. Draper

Yours of 14th to hand. We were much surprized at the contents as we were not aware of any arrangement with you by Miss Doddridge. Some weeks since Miss D. offer the books to us and we agreed to publish it. The proper way now is we think for you to correspond with her & we are ready to do whatever is right on the premises. It is proper for us to say that the work has not yet been commence by us. With kind regards to self & wife, I am yours truly

G. W. Remsen

over

My family are in usual health but just now very much worn out both Daughter & Mrs. R. as we have just burried my son John aged 28 year, of Disease of the throat strings he was confined to the room about 6 weeks but passed away very peacefully.

[p. 107]
Letters from N. Doddridge to L. C. Draper

Wellsburg, July 7, 1869

L. C. Draper, Esq.

Yours of 2 inst. to hand. I have just enclosed your last letter, to my brother, J. G. Doddridge, with a view of having his opinion in regard to your recent determination to put "Doddridge's Notes" under cover with "Withers' Chronicles of Border Warfare".

When I hear from him, will write again.

Pleas make my respectful regards to Mr. Croffert.

Respectfully yours,

N. Doddridge.

Wellsburg, July 19, 1869

L. C. Draper, Esq.

I wrote you briefly on the 3d, intending after due reflection on the subject to give a final answer to the proposal contained in your communication of the 2 inst.

You are aware that your present arrangement for bringing out the "Notes", under cover with another book, is entirely foreign to the one proposed when you received permission to Edit and republish them; and, in my opinion, it is one which you were not warranted in making without my approbation. Your arrangement is extremely distasteful to me and one to which I can in no wise give my consent, nor would I now be willing to have any notes appended to the original without knowing their purport; hence, in the future, I wish you to consider that you have no authority or control over "Doddridge's Notes."

It is a source of gratification to me to know that, as Mr. Withers' work is on a similar subject with the Notes, you will have a field in which to use the annotations you may have prepared, so they will not be lost.

In your letter of Feb. 1866, you said, "It was of no moment to you to Edit the "Notes", except so far as it might give you some reputation as a careful Western historical Antiquary." This reputation you have already attained, and whether the Editing ... works, other than your own, is necessary to establish it, is questionable.

I do not regard you as mercenary or ungenerous, and hope not to give offence by saying that if you will give me an account of the different sieges at Wheeling, and any other matter that will add interest to the "Notes", altho' I am poor, I will make a reasonable compensation, and also give you due credit for them.

[p. 108]
Please Accept my thanks for a copy of the very interesting address of Hon. N. S. Orton.

Truly yours,
N. Doddridge

[p. 109]
Memorandum from L. C. Draper to N. Doddridge

Memo July 2d 69.
    To Miss Doddridge.
  Offered her 2 pr. cent of my 7 & 1 per cent of Mr. Crofferts 5, on the relative proportion of the "Notes" to the whole work, in one cover, of Doddridge & Withers &c. That in one cover, it wd. warrant canvassing for — singly it wd. not — & thus a much larger profit would accrue to her than if pubd. in the ordinary way.
  That we wd. promise to have the work in publishers hands by or during the ensuring Spring, & may be it wd. be issued by that time, as the publishers are Enterprising, & Mr. C. & I will give it all our Efforts to hasten its publication. Wd. make a written contract, Mr. C & I, or publishers, or both parties, & she have her percentage Every 6 months.
  If she desired it, cd. have such teritory in her region as she cd. canvass, & books at lowest wholesale price, & probably cd. make from a dollar to a dollar & a half on a vol for canvassing & delivery.

[p. 109[1]]
To Miss Doddridge
Offer abt. republishing Doddridge's Notes.
July 2d 69

Printed notice

State Historical Society of Wisconsin.
Madison, Wis. _____ 1854.

Sir:

It is my pleasing duty to inform you, that at a meeting of the Executive Committee, you were duly elected a _____ Member of the STATE HISTORICAL SOCIETY OF WISCONSIN.

Should such membership be agreeable to you, you will please signify the same by letter, as early as convenient.

The objects and wishes of the Society are briefly set forth in the annexed Circular.

I remain, with great respect,

Your obedient servant,

Corresponding Secretary.

Active members pay an annual fee of one dollar; twenty dollars, paid at one time, constitutes the donor a life member; while honorary and corresponding members are exempt from fee or taxation.

INDEXING NOTE

Page numbers used as locators in the index refer to those written on the pages of the original manuscript, which appear in the microfilmed edition of the manuscript of Volume 1ZZ. These numbers also correspond to the page numbers appearing in brackets in the transcript.

Every occurrence of all personal names appearing in Volume 1ZZ is indexed, using last, first, and middle names when available. When only a last name is used in the manuscript, the first name is supplied in brackets when it can be determined with reasonable certainty from other sources. Certain persons identified only by title in the manuscript are indexed by name, with the full name given in brackets. Titles such as military rank, academic degree, or political office are used with personal names only if no given name is provided in the manuscript, or to avoid confusion with other persons having the same name. If neither given name nor title is available, the person is indexed as e.g. Mr. or Mrs. at the surname, with any identifying information in the modifier.

The original spellings of personal and place names are preserved in the transcription. Such spellings frequently vary. In the index, spellings of these names are normalized to the most commonly occurring variants of the full names, with alternate spellings being given in parentheses at the main heading for the name. Other variant spellings of names, if these appear elsewhere in the alphabetically arranged index, are cross-referred to the main heading for the name. (Double posting is used for variant spellings of infrequently occurring names.) Word-by-word sorting has been employed in ordering the index headings.

INDEX

A

Academy of Natural Sciences (Philadelphia, Pa.), 24
Adams, Mr., of Tuscaloosa Falls, Ala., 84
adoption of prisoners by Indians, 49
Adory, W., of Tuscaloosa Falls, Ala., 87
Albach, [James R.], 96
Allen, [Hugh], killed in battle of Point Pleasant, W. Va. (1774), 34[10]
ambition, religion as outlet for, in United States, 38
American Express Co., printed receipt, 90
Americans, freedom of, 38
angekoks (angikoks) (sorcerers in Greenland), 71, 76
animals
    around Old Mingo Towns, Ohio, as food source, 54, 55
    imitation of sounds of, by Indians, 59, 60
Annals of the West, by James H. Perkins, 32
Arbuckle, Mathew, 34[6]
architecture of court house (Bedford, Penn.), 6, 7, 33[7]
Asbury, Francis, 17
astronomy, use by Indians, 60

B

backwoodsmen, dress and habits of, 90
battle cries of Indians, 59
battle of Point Pleasant, W. Va. (1774), 34[8]–34[12]
Bausman, Mr., of Brownsville, Penn., 4
Beane, Mr., of Tuscaloosa Falls, Ala., 45
beans as Indian food source, 55
Bedford, Penn., architecture of court house, 33[4]
Bedford Spring, Penn., description of, 5, 6, 33[5], 33[6]
beekeeping, 26, 28, 29
bees, migration of, 72
Benham, [Joseph S.] (attorney), 46
Benjeman (Bingeman), John, 36
Biggs, Benjamin, letters to, 42–44
Bingeman (Benjeman), John, 36
Bird, Mr. (lawyer, Bedford, Penn.), 7
Bissel, [John N.], history of England by, 34[13]
bogberry, 45, 76
Bond, Col. (officer of court in Columbus, Ohio), 46
Boone
    Dl., 90
    Wm. F., 9
Boquet (Boquett, Bouquett), [Henri], 34[4], 74
Bowers, Rev., 73
Braddock, [Edward], 73
Bradstreet, [John], 74
Brady
    I., 94, 102
    Samuel, 33[1], 95
Brannan
    B. F., 33[12]
    Mary D., 33[12]
Brashier(s), [Basil], of Brownsville, Penn., 4
Brice family (West Liberty, Penn.), 44

Brooke Co., W. Va., Joseph Doddridge as magistrate of, 24
Brown, Ellen D., 15, 39
Browne, Mr., of Tuscaloosa Falls, Ala., 45
Buck (Bucke), David, 77, 81, 82, 85
buckberry, 45, 72, 76
Buckengehelas (Indian), 75
Buford, Thomas, 34^7, 34^{10}
Bukey
    Hezekiah, 33^1
    Jemima, 33^1, 101
    John, 33^1, 95
    Maria, 33^1
    Mary, 33^1
    Rudolph, 33^1
    Wm., 93, 95
burial of Indians in cavern, 54
Butler, Mann, 31, 32
    opinion of Doddridge's *Notes*, 9

C

Caldwell, James, 43
Calvinists, fragmentation of, in United States, 38
Campbell
    Alexander, 8
    Mr. (teacher of Joseph Doddridge), 27
Carneal, Mr., 46
Carothers, [Moses], 93
Carson, Ruth, 39
Carswell, Mr. (attorney), 46
cavern as Indian burial site, 54
Chambers, Dd., 69
Chapline, I., 43
Chase, [Philander], 33^7
Childress, James, 84
Chips, Mr., indictment of, in Morgantown, W. Va. (1796), 42
Christian, William, 34^7, 34^{10}
Cisney (Cissna), Mr., of Cumberland Co., Penn., 6, 33^7
Clark, Col., 75
Claxton, Edmund, 106
Clay, [William Mitchell], killed by Indians (1774), 34^{10}, 34^{11}
Clendennen (Clindennen), Archibald, 34^3

clothing of Indians, 55, 58, 59
Collins, [Lewis], 32
Collins, Mrs. (niece of Joseph Doddridge), 33^9
Condry, Isaac, 79, 86
Conium maculatum (poison root), use by Indians as purgative, 64
Constitutional Convention of Virginia (1829-1830), 8
convicts, 74
copper implements of Indians, 71
corn as Indian food source, 55, 57
Cornstalk (Indian), 34^{10}, 34^{11}, 69
cotton, shipment of bales of, 45, 77–88
council house in Indian village, 57, 58
Coward, Mr., in battle with Indians, 34^{10}, 34^{11}
Cox
    B., 83
    G., 83
Craig, [Neville B.], 32
cranberry, 45, 76
Crawford, [William], 73
Cresap, [Michael]., 95
Croffert, Wm. A., 1, 107, 109
Croft, Wm. S., 77, 78, 83, 85
Cruger, [Lydia], 94, 99, 101, 102

D

Dalzell, Mr., 74
dances, ceremonial, of Indians, 65, 66
Day, Sherman, *Historical Collections of Pennsylvania* by, 32
death, anticipation of, by Joseph Doddridge, 4, 5
Delaware Indians in battle of Point Pleasant, W. Va. (1774), 34^{11}
Delft, 73
dhoura bread, 73
"Dialogue between a Dandy and a Backwoodsman," by Joseph Doddridge, 33^4
Dickinson, John, 34^6
dictionaries of Indian languages, 71
Dillen, Lt., killed in battle of Point Pleasant, W. Va. (1774), 34^{10}
Dillon, [John Brown], 32
Dillon's Hotel or Tavern (Bedford, Penn.), 6, 33^5

District of Columbia, codification of laws of, 8
Doddridge
  Ann, 13
  Charles Hammond, 27, 33[12]
  E., 43
  Eliza M., elegy to, 11, 40[1]
  Ellen, 15, 39
  Harriet T., 27, 33[12]
  J. G. (brother of Narcissa), 91, 92, 107
  Jemima, 25, 33[1], 101
    letters to, 4–7
  John, 13, 17, 39, 39[3], 95
  Joseph (1769-1826), 39[4], 95, 101
    biography of, 13–25, 28–31
    character of, 10, 15, 19, 33[2], 33[3]
    death of, 33[12]
    letters from, 3–7
    Notes on the Settlement & Indian Wars of the Western Parts of Virginia and Pennsylvania (See *Notes on the Settlement...*, by Joseph Doddridge)
  Joseph (died 1779), foreman of grand jury (Bedford, Penn., 1777), 33[6]
  Mary D., 5, 6, 27, 33[12]
  Mary (Wells), 13
  Narcissa, 7, 10, 106
    letters from, 91–95, 97–105, 107
    memoir of Rev. Joseph Doddridge, 33[1]
  Philip (1702-1751), 13, 14
  Philip (1772-1832), 18, 19, 33[12], 90
    biography of, 8
    death of, 9
    letter to John C. Wright, 46
    letters to Benjamin Biggs, 42–44
  Philip (born 1793), 95
  Philip (brother of John), 16, 90
    capture of family of, by Wyandot Indians (1778), 39–39[4], 94
  Philip Bukey (1795-1860), 101
    letters to, 3, 4, 25
    obituary of, 47
  R. Reeves (Rezin), 4-7, 27
    death of, 33[8]–33[10]
    elegy to, 12, 41
Doddridge *(Continued)*
  S. (daughter of Joseph), 26
  Doddridge's *Notes. See Notes on the Settlement...*, by Joseph Doddridge
Donaldson, Charles, 42
Drake, [Benjamin], 32
Draper, Lyman C., 90
  new edition of Doddridge's *Notes* planned by, 1
drums, use in Indian ceremonial dances, 65
Dunkard, Mrs. Glass rescued by a young, 72
Dunmore, Lord (John Murray)
  escape from Williamsburg, Va., 34[17]
  expedition against Shawnee Indians, 34[5]–34[12], 75
Duval (Duvall)
  Edward, 4
  Harriet T., 27, 33[12]
  Wm., 33[12]

E

Easten, Mr., of Tuscaloosa Falls, Ala., 83
Edgington, Thos., 72, 73
education
  of Indian children, 59–61
  religious, Philip B. Doddridge activity in, 47
Egyptian dhoura bread, 73
Egyptian superscriptions, 71
England, colonization of Virginia by, 49
Epaminondas, 71
epicacuanha (ipecacuanha), 73
Episcopal Church
  history of, in United States, 10, 91, 104
  joined by Joseph Doddridge, 19
  parishes headed by Joseph Doddridge, 20, 22, 23, 33[7], 33[8], 33[10]
execution of prisoners by Indians, 49

F

Fair, Adam, 45, 80
feast of expiation among Indians, 64, 65

Fields, John, 34[5], 34[7], 34[10], 34[11]
Finley, James B., 39[4], 95
firearms, use by Indians, 58, 59
Fisk, Mr., 73
Flag, Peter, 34[12]
Fleming
  J. W., 69
  Wm., 34[6], 34[9]
Forbes, [John], 34[14], 34[15]
foresters, dress and habits of, 90
Fort Laurens, Ohio, 75
Fort Pitt, Pennsylvania, 75
Fox, Mr. (attorney), 46
funeral, Philip Doddridge extraordinary duties at, 24

G

Galarpec, Mr., 87
Galaspie (Gillespie), M. H., 45
Galitzer, letters to, by "Russian Spy," 37, 38
game around Old Mingo Towns, Ohio, 54, 55
Gass, Patrick, 97, 102
[Gayoso de Lemos, Manuel], Spanish governor of Natchez, 8
genealogy of Joseph Doddridge, 13, 14
  search for, 6
German language, Joseph Doddridge mastery of, 17
Gillespie (Galaspie), M. H., 45
Glass, Mrs., rescued by a young Dunkard, 72
Goldsby, Lt., killed in battle of Point Pleasant, W. Va. (1774), 34[10]
Goode
  Joseph, 45
  Thomas, 45
Gooding, J., 43
Gorman, W., 87
Grant, William, 74
  in attack on Fort Du Quesne, Penn., 34[14]–34[16]
Grave Creek Mound, 71
Greathouse
  Harmon, 33[1]
  Maria, 33[1]
Greece, revolution in (1823-1824), 71
Greenbrier Co., W. Va., early history of, 34[2]–34[4]
Greenbrier River, W. Va., exploration of, 34–34[3]
Greenland, sorcerers in, 76
Grigsby, [Hugh Blair], 8
Gulan's Leap, 90
guns, use by Indians, 58, 59

H

Haffelfinger, C. C., 106
Hains, Joseph, 34[6]
Hall, [James], *Sketches of the West* by, 31
Hallitt, T. L., 78–80
Hammond, [Charles] (attorney), 46
Hammonds, Capt., of Tuscaloosa Falls, Ala., 78, 79
Hardie, Mr. (hermit), 93
Harris, M. M., 83
Harrison
  Benjn., 34[6]
  J., 43
Hart, [Adolphus Mordecai], 32
Hartley, [Cecil B.], 32
De Hass, [Wills.], *History and Indian Wars of Western Virginia* by, 32
Hendrick, Gustavus, 78, 80, 86
Herbert, [William], in battle of Point Pleasant, W. Va. (1774), 34[7]
Highlanders defeated at Fort Du Quesne, Penn. (1755), 34[14]
Hildreth, [Samuel Prescott], 32
Historical Collections of Pennsylvania, by Sherman Day, 32
Historical Collections of Virginia and Ohio, by Henry Howe, 32
History and Indian Wars of Western Virginia, by Wills. de Hass, 32
History of the Valley of the Mississippi, by John W. Monette, 32
history of western Virginia and Pennsylvania, 30, 31
Hogg, Capt., French surveyor killed by (1753), 34[13]
Howe, [Henry], *Historical Collections of Virginia and Ohio* by, 32
Howison, [Robert Reid], 32
Hunt, Wm., 34[6]

Hutton, Troy, 83

I

imitation of animal sounds by Indians, 59, 60
impartiality required of journalists, 37
indentured servants, 74
Indiana, proposed State of, land sale announced in (1776), 2
Indians. *See also* individual tribes
    attack by
        at Point Pleasant, W. Va. (1774), 34^8–34^{12}
        on settlers in Greenbrier County, Va. (1763), 34^3
    copper implements and languages of, 71
    independent spirit of, 49, 50
Indians *(Continued)*
    prayers of, 66–69
    Six Nations, treaty with, at Ft. Stanwick, N. Y. (1768), 34^{16}
    victory at Fort Du Quesne, Penn. (1755), 34^{14}
    wars with, in Pennsylvania and western Virginia, history of, 30, 31
industriousness prized by Joseph Doddridge, 3
injustice of life bemoaned by journalist, 37
ipecacuanha (epicacuanha), 73

J

Jacob
    J. G., 95
    John J., 17
    S., 95
Jacobs, [J. A.], 32
Jefferson Academy (Canonsburg, Penn.), 18, 19
Jenkins, Mr., of Tuscaloosa Falls, Ala., 88
Johnson, David, 18
journalists, skills required of, 37
Junenville, Mr., killed at Little Meadows, Penn. (1753), 34^{13}

K

Kellogg, [Ezra B.], 47
Kelly, Walter, 34^5
Kercheval, [Samuel], 32
Keywood, Mr., of Tuscaloosa Falls, Ala., 45
Kinnekenick, 71
Kirby, Mr., of Tuscaloosa Falls, Ala., 83
Kirk, Mrs., 93, 95

L

Laidley, W. S., 90
Lane, N., 43
languages of Indians, 71
Laurel Hill, Penn., description of, 4
Leaven, G. B., 77, 80-82, 86
Lee, Henry, 10, 101, 102
Leigh, [Benjamin Watkins], 8
Lewis
    Andrew
        in battle of Point Pleasant, W. Va. (1774), 34^{11}, 34^{12}
        in French and Indian War, 34^{14}–34^{17}
        in Lord Dunmore's War (1774), 34–34^4, 34^6–34^8
        wounded at Little Meadows, Penn. (1753), 34^{13}
    Charles, 34^4, 34^6, 34^9, 34^{10}
    John, 34^3, 34^6
Linsley, Mr., 43
"Literature of the West," paper by James H. Perkins, 32
Little Meadows, Penn., battle of (1753), 34^{13}
"Logan, the last of the race of Shikellemus — a dramatic piece," by Joseph Doddridge, 33^4
Lord Dunmore's War, 34^5–34^{12}, 75
Lutherans, fragmentation of, in United States, 38
Lyon (Lyons), Mr. (lawyer, Brownsville, Penn.), 4

M

McClenachan
  Alexander, 34[6]
  Robert, 34[6], 34[10]
McCollach (McColloch)
  John, 33[1], 93, 95
  Mary, 33[1]
  [Samuel]
    in battle of Point Pleasant, W. Va. (1774), 34[8]
    leap by (Wheeling, W. Va., 1777), 93, 95
McDonald
  Angus, 74, 75
  John, 32, 98, 101
McGuire, Maj., favors saving Moravians, 75
McKeever, Mr., 43
M'Kiernan, [George S.], 91
McMahon, Wm., 33[1]
McMillen, John, 74
Maneto (Manito, Manitou), worship of, by Indians, 58, 66, 67
Martin
  Jacob, 34, 34[2]
  Mr., judgment against (1804), 43
Mathews
  George, 34[6]
  Sam., 34[17]
Mayer, [Frank Blackwell], 32
Mayfield, Micajah, 45
medicine studied by Joseph Doddridge, 21, 33[1]
Mercer, Rev., at Jefferson Academy (Canonsburg, Pa.), 18
Metcalf (Mitcelf), Geo., 43
meteorology, use by Indians, 60
Methodist Church, 16, 19
migration of bees and settlers, coordinated, 72
mineral springs near Brownsville, Penn., 4
Mingo Towns, settlement of, 53
Mitcelf (Metcalf), Geo., 43
Monette, [John Wesley], *History of the Valley of the Mississippi* by, 32
Moore
  Ann, 13
  Mr., 43

Moravians at Fort Pitt, Penn. (1781), 75
Morgan, George, 2
[Murray, John] (Lord Dunmore), expedition against Shawnee Indians, 34[5]–34[12]
Murray (Murrey), John (Capt.), 34[6], 34[10]
music, Joseph Doddridge love of, 33[3]

N

Nagel (Nagle), Mr. (landlord, Bedford, Penn.), 6, 33[5]
Nall, Mr., bitten by mad wolf, 72
Nash, E., 79
Natchez, Tenn., Spanish governor of, dines with Philip Doddridge, 8
nature, Joseph Doddridge's love of, 25, 26, 28
negotiation, art of, among Indians, 60
Notes on the Settlement & Indian Wars of the Western Parts of Virginia and Pennsylvania, by Joseph Doddridge, 1, 10, 29–31, 33[4], 95
  notes and references for new edition of, 69–76
  proposal for new edition of, 91, 94, 103, 105, 107, 109
  sale of, 6
Nuza (fictional Indian), 59, 61–63

O

Ohio River, white settlements on (1771), 72
Old Mingo Towns on Ohio River, settlement of, 53
Oma (fictional Indian), 59–63
oratory, Philip Doddridge lack of skill in, 8
Orton, N. S., 108
Oxycoccus, 76

P

paper, tax on, effect on publishing, 94
Parkman, [Francis], 32
patriotism of Indians to their heritage, 50–52

Patterson, Robert, 18
Paxton massacre (Lancaster, Penn., 1763), 74
Peck, John M., 32
  Life of Boone by, 96
Perkins, James H., *Annals of the West* by, 32
Phillips, Mr., of Tuscaloosa Falls, Ala., 85
picture writing of Indians, 71
plantain, 73
Point Pleasant, W. Va., 73
  battle of (1774), 34^8–34^{12}
poison root (Conium maculatum), use by Indians as purgative, 64
Pontius, Tomlinson, 69
Potter, Thomas, 45
Powhatan confederacy of Indian nations, 53
prayers of Indians, 66–69
printing materials, tax on, effect on publishing, 94
prisoners, adoption or execution by Indians, 49
proselytization by American churches, 38
Protestant Episcopal Church. *See* Episcopal Church
purgatives, ceremonial use by Indians, 64

Q

Quinn, James, 16, 95

R

rabies from bite by mad wolf, 72
Raleigh, Walter, 49
Randolph
  Drake F., 80, 82
  [John], role in Virginia Constitutional Convention (1829-1830), 8
rattles, use in Indian ceremonial dances, 65
rattlesnake bites, 72
Reeves, Nathan, Mrs., 33^{10}
Relfe, [John], attorney in Morgantown, W. Va., 42
religion as outlet for ambition, 38
Rempson, P., 88

Remsen
  George W., 106
  John, 106
  Peter A., 45
representative government of United States, essay on, 38
retribution lands (West Virginia), announcement of sale of (1776), 2
Rice's Fort (Washington Co., Penn.), attack on (1781), 105
roads in Pennsylvania, deplorable condition of, 5
Robunload, Levi, 45
Rooney, Ms., 73
Rowland, Thos., 34^6
Rush, Benj., 21
Russell, Benjn., 69
"Russian spy," 92–94
  letters from, 37, 38
Rutherford, Mr., of Tuscaloosa Falls. Ala., 84, 88

S

Saltonstall, G., 87
Sandwich Islands, 71
Schoolcraft, [H. R.], 32, 71
Scots Highlanders defeated at Fort Du Quesne, Penn. (1755), 34^{14}
Scott, Thomas, 17, 33^{10}, 93
service tree, 72
settlement
  of frontier, migration of bees coordinated with, 72
  of western Virginia and Pennsylvania, 30, 31
settlers
  in Greenbrier Co., Va., attacked by Indians (1763), 34^3
  ordered to vacate western Virginia (1761), 34^2
Sewell, Stephen, 34, 34^2
Shaw, I., 79
Shawnee Indians in battle of Point Pleasant, W. Va. (1774), 34^{11}
Sheffield, Mr., of Tuscaloosa Falls, Ala., 77, 80–82

Shelby
  Evan, 34[7]
  Tho., 69
Shelton, Mr., of Tuscaloosa Falls, Ala., 88
Singer, Mrs., bitten by rattlesnake, 72
Six Nations of Indians, treaty with, at Ft. Stanwick, N. Y. (1768), 34[16]
Sketches of the West, by James Hall, 31
Slauter, Mr., of Tuscaloosa Falls, Ala., 87
Smith
  [Amanda], *Travels in America* by, 34[17]
  Ballard, 34[3]
  Josh., 74
snake bites, 72, 73
sorcerers in Greenland, 76
South Sea dream, 72
Southern Literary Messenger, 90
Sparks, Mr., of Tuscaloosa Falls, Ala., 88
speaking ability of Joseph Doddridge, 33[10]
spirits (liquor), poisonous reptile bites treatment with, 73
squash as Indian food source, 55
St. Clair, [Arthur], 73
stagnant water, illnesses blamed on, 5, 6
Stanard, [Robert], 8
State Historical Society of Wisconsin, 109
Steelman, Mr., of Tuscaloosa Falls, Ala., 87
Stevens, [Edward], 34[17]
Stewart (Stuart)
  Col., 95
  John, 34[6], 35
  Mr., of Tuscaloosa Falls, Alabama, 87
Stone, [Frederick Dawson], 32
Stuart (Stewart)
  Col., 95
  John, 34[6], 35
  Mr., of Tuscaloosa Falls, Alabama, 87
sun
  Indian prayer to, 68, 69
  usefulness of working by light of, 3

T

Tancrue, Rowland, 81
Tarrence, Mr., of Tuscaloosa Falls, Alabama, 88
taxes on paper and printing materials, 94
Taylor
  [James Wickes], 24, 32
  Penn, 77, 80–82
Tazewell, [Littleton Waller], 8
temperance movement, 47
temperature in summer since 1824, 72
Teter, Samuel, 93, 95, 101
  bear adventure, 71
  brother-in-law of John and Philip Doddridge, 16, 97
  hunting camp of, 73
  sale of farm, 39[3]
Thomas, John, 79, 81, 86
Thompson, Mr., of Tuscaloosa Falls, Alabama, 82
toad, plantain eaten by, 73
Tomlinson
  A. D., 71
  Joseph, 33[1]
Treatise on the Culture of Bees, by Joseph Doddridge, 29
treaty with Six Nations of Indians at Ft. Stanwick, N. Y. (1768), 34[16]
Truss, W., 87
Turkey, Greek war of independence from (1823-1824), 71
Tuscaloosa Falls, Ala., as center of cotton trade, 45, 79–88
Tutela (Indian novel), by Joseph Doddridge, 48–69

U

unification of Indians against whites, proposal for, 61, 62
Upshur, [Abel Parker], 8

V

Van Metre, Mr., 69
vegetables cultivated by Indians, 55, 57
Vernon, Maj., 75
Virginia
   colonization by England, 49
   Constitutional Convention (1829-1830), 8
   settlers ordered to vacate western part of (1761), 34^2

W

wagon, repair of axle on, 5
Walker
   Mr., 70
   Thos., 34^{16}
wall-ink, 73
Wallace
   Mr., 93
   Robert, 97, 98
wampum belts, 60
Wappatonika Campaign, 75
Ward, James, 34^6, 34^{10}
Washington, George, 34^{12}–34^{14}, 34^{17}
Waugh, Miss, marries lawyer Bird (Bedford, Penn.), 7
weapons of Indians, 58–60
Wells
   Alex., 72
   Cynthia, 101
   M. S., 75
   Mary, 13, 15
   Mr. (uncle of Joseph Doddridge), 5
   Richard, 95
   Ths., 72
Wesleyan Methodist Society, 16, 19
Wetzel
   Jac., 75
   M., 75
Wheeling, W. Va., sieges of, 91
White, [William], bishop of Episcopal Church in Philadelphia, 21–23
wigwams, construction of, 55
wildlife around Old Mingo Towns, Ohio, as food source, 54, 55
Williams, John W., 79
Williamson, [David], 75
Wilson, Saml., 34^6, 34^{10}

Winnepeck (Winnepick) Indians, 53, 55
Wisconsin, State Historical Society of, 109
Withers, [Alexander Scott], 32, 91
   Chronicles of Border Warfare by, 107
wolf, bite by mad, 72
Wolf, Mr. (friend of M. Wetzel), 75
Wood, John, 84, 88
Wright, John C., letter from Philip Doddridge, 46
writing, wampum belts as form of, 60
Wyandot Indians
   in battle of Point Pleasant, W. Va. (1774), 34^{11}
   Doddridge family capture by, 39–39^2

Y

yells of Indians, types of, 59

Z

Zane, Noah, 70, 105
Zanesville, Ohio, Episcopal parish founded by Joseph Doddridge, 22, 33^7, 33^8, 33^{10}

www.ingramcontent.com/pod-product-compliance
Lightning Source LLC
Chambersburg PA
CBHW071207160426
43196CB00011B/2216